Absolute Sovereignty of the People

Absolute Sovereignty of The People

2011
Aquila Press, Inc.

Trafford rev. 08/25/2011

 www.trafford.com

North America & International
toll-free: 1 888 232 4444 (USA & Canada)
phone: 250 383 6864 ♦ fax: 812 355 4082

Dedication

This book is dedicated to my brother, Walt, who had only an elementary grade schooling, due to the need to assist our widowed mother during the Great Depression of the 1930s, but self-taught himself in developing beliefs and goals that he espoused, relentlessly and uncompromisingly, challenging the usurped economic and political power of the time.

As a candidate in races for Mayor and for the United States Congress, he stressed at all times the "absolute sovereignty" of the people. He knew that merely pledging belief in the sovereignty of the people was only a rhetorical expression. It was actually exercising supreme power in a role of decision-making that gave "sovereignty" vitality and political reality.

Adelaide and I, as co-editors of *The Eagle's Eye,* will eternally be thankful for his unswerving and dedicated role as our researcher and political analyst.

Contents

Preface

THERE is no way that this nation can be restored to a state of economic fairness and non-violence without the people exercising their absolute sovereign power, both economically and politically! To date they have left their well being and destiny in the hands of predatory and despotic corporate entities that have landed the nation into its current dilemma of trillions of dollars in public and private debt, millions homeless, tens of millions without jobs and health insurance, and tens of millions with troubled minds. We have become a nation unanchored, without compass, morally and spiritually bankrupt!

In re-reading copies of *The Eagle's Eye*, which we published during the 1960s, we are startled to see how accurately the conclusions and projections of that time define what we are enduring today. What registers so clearly in our minds is that the intolerable conditions a half century ago, caused by the malfunctioning of our economic, financial and political systems, are the same wrongly structured frameworks responsible for the current hardships and suffering that now persist throughout the land.

Why has it taken us so long to not recognize our faulty systems **themselves** in conducting our nation's business and consequently are inability to meet the citizen's most serious human needs? Most seriously, why have we tolerated a policy and an economy of cold and hot wars, sacrificing our young, when neither our security nor self-interests were at stake?

In *There Is A Way!* I wrote, "Some two thousand years ago, a most dynamic, but humble personality, walked the shores of Galilee beseeching the people to treat others the way that they themselves wished to be treated, to be just and compassionate, and be sensitive to the ills and burdens of others.

"To those in power He was a troublemaker, a revolutionist, one guilty of sedition, and one who sought to 'tip over existing institutions'. However, He was not deterred by all charges and threats to his person. He had a mission to fulfill.

"Can you envision Him meekly accepting the status quo? Do you believe that He would consider the 'Pharisees' and 'Sanhedrin' of today too formidable to be confronted? Would he be simply satisfied to preach a future day of 'heavenly bliss' and let time erase all earthly pain?

"Isn't it more likely that He would unequivocally and unflinchingly indict the exploiters and defilers of all that was wholesome and just? That He would show no toleration of all conditions and actions that caused such an endless stream of victims, particularly innocent children? That He would find unacceptable a socio-economic system that actually spawned violence and caused widespread want?

"Doesn't it seem most natural that, as of yore, He would fashion a 'scourge of cords' and rally the people to drive the 'money-changers out of the Temple'?

"He challenged us, 'If you believe in Me, pick up your cross and follow Me!' He, then, most faithfully projected, 'Ye shall know the truth and the truth shall set you free!' This is the challenge we face! Are we prepared, in mind and heart, to accept it?"

In 2010, our corporation, Aquila Press, Inc., published *A Reluctant Heretic* by Adelaide Pelley Pearson in which she wrote 71 editorials for our magazine, *The Eagle's Eye*. Her succinct and analytical thinking resonated with all who read her editorials. We feel that similar appreciation will be accorded the feature articles in the magazine, which we are now reprinting.

Adelaide and I were mortal partners for 62 years and we were co-editors of *The Eagle's Eye,* which Aquila published during the hectic times of the 1960s.

The first article we are re-printing is "The Manipulated Mystery of Money" which appeared in the April 1963 issue. We have chosen this article because there is no economic force in our society that impacts so acutely and devastatingly on our lives as private banking control of the nation's credit and money.

Subsequent articles, in candor and substance, are equally relevant for our consideration. Their enlightenment is also imperative if the nation is to endure and survive!

Mel Pearson
March 12, 2011

~ 1 ~

Manipulated Mystery
Of Money

WALK UP to the average person, struggling to pay his bills, and keep his family clothed, fed and sheltered, and announce to him that you have just placed $5,000 to his checking account in the local bank. Tell him that there are no strings attached to this gesture and henceforth he is free to spend it as he sees fit.

If you are successful in convincing him that he is not the victim of trickery or some fraudulent scheme, you will have satisfied the one and only basic concern of the average American respecting the whole subject called "money." You will have provided him with "purchasing power."

Purchasing Power! It is the common denominator of all economic systems. It is the weakness and strength of all such systems. In practical terms it means the kind of food on your table, the kind of home you live in, the kind of car you drive, and the kind of medical care and education you can provide for your family.

No, it is not difficult to understand that money, or purchasing power, whether in the form of cash or checking account, is the most important concern in the day-to-day life of each citizen trying to work out his security and well being.

"All I want to do is get my hands on plenty of that green stuff," is the urge expressed by every hard-pressed citizen.

What is difficult to understand is that such hard-pressed citizen evinces so little real interest or concern in basically understanding *how* and *why* the "green stuff" seems to be at such high premium and *what* in the final analysis should be the true role of money as translated into a nation's purchasing power. And yet there is a reason for such lack of real interest.

HE has been conditioned to conclude that the whole money subject is too complex and esoteric for his feeble brain to comprehend. Just one glance at the latest statistical report of the Federal Reserve Bank and he is convinced of his conclusion. He accepts, naively, that an understanding of "money" is indeed reserved for bankers!

The tragedy of such a state of mind is that Federal Reserve statistical reports, compound-interest tabulations, and the one hundred and one forms of loans and mortgages, all liens against the future, have nothing to do whatsoever with a basic understanding of the proper functioning of money as purchasing power in a constructive economy. These are all ramifications of the malfunctioning of a nation's medium of exchange.

EVEN more tragic is the fact that the average person is unaware that the complexities and mysteries enshrouding the whole subject of money have been purposely created with premeditated design, that the economic and financial enslavement of all citizens might go undetected. The nation's usurers want no obstruction to their merry game of perpetually extracting their "pound of flesh" notwithstanding resultant wholesale suffering and the sacrifice of life itself. After all, have they not been getting away with it for thousands of years?

Once again the time has come to drive "the money-changers from the temple." But this time it must be done so that there can be no recurrence of the malpractices that can reduce an entire nation to a state of hopeless bondage. This can be accomplished by erecting an economic framework within which usury, loans, and all liens against man's future earnings are eliminated simply because they are archaic, evil and unworkable.

We don't need the money merchant with his bags of gold and silver discs, not to mention the whole superfluous mechanism of creating fictitious credit, which have "gummed up" economics for centuries. The nation can breathe, think, and enjoy life much more wholesomely and prosperously without them!

It is not the purpose of this article to present a detailed picture of the intricate workings of privately owned banking interests and the usurped powers they arbitrarily exercise to the detriment of the entire economy. In other booklets and articles we have challenged the soundness of any system, which permits non-governmental institutions to create "fictitious credit" and to destroy the value of human effort by arbitrary expansion and contraction of such credit.

We have endeavored to show how the entire load of astronomical indebtedness, now exceeding *two trillion dollars* under which the nation founders, is the direct result of a monetary system which is premised on debt

19

and which permits the credit of the United states to be exploited by voracious monied interests.

WE WILL continue to make these charges and challenges. At the same time, we realize that while such a position and action do serve to emphasize the injustice of our monetary practice and the seriousness of our economic instability, they do not clearly portray the shortcomings of the system as a system. This can only be appreciated and unmistakably grasped by understanding what role money should play in an honest and constructive economy. It is then that the faults and fallacies of the current role of money, or the nation's medium of exchange, become glaringly evident.

As we mentioned in the start of this article, the average person expresses no concern about money than that he will acquiesce to any program that will give him more of that "green stuff." In short, he is simply stating, "Increase my purchasing power so I can buy the things my family needs, both as to necessities and comforts, and I'm with you!" With this thought in mind as a common jumping-off point for all Americans, let us consider a hypothetical situation, which should clarify our fundamental thinking about the whole subject.

Quoting directly from *No More Hunger,* page 82, which deals with the question of where the dividends, or "money," come from with which to underwrite or carry on the nation's business under a Cooperative Commonwealth, we find:

"SUPPOSE we consider the United States as a absolute island. Instead of Canada on the north, suppose there was only ocean, and the same with

Mexico on the south. Further, suppose that there was no other land area above water on the surface of the globe, that America was one island, one country, one nation.

"Now on that single continent-island are marooned 180,000,000 persons. There are 108 million adults and 72 million children. Of that 108 million adults, 54 million are women, keeping their homes, bearing their youngsters and caring for their menfolk. Of that 54 million men, some are carpenters, some are miners, some are farmers, some are manufacturers, some are professional men, but each has his chore to perform for all the rest of the islanders, no matter how grandiose his compensation.

Very good! Now suppose they all 'duff in' and do their work. But there is not a single gold or silver dollar in all the island, nor has one ever been conceived or manufactured. Some way must be found to divide up all the goods so that each gets his fair share of the total production, according to his industry and talent.

"What better way could there be, I ask you, than for the management of the island to keep a book account of what each man has done, what its value is in relation to the whole production, and how such goods should be allotted to him in consequence? Only, instead of actually dividing up the literal goods and making compensations 'n kind,' as payment in goods is expressed, suppose that all the workers have placed to their common credit in a bank the total value of that composite production for a given year. They can buy, or not buy, any kind of goods they choose, but buy and consume all they ultimately must, in the very nature of

21

things, or cease making the kinds of goods which nobody consumes.

"Now then, break down that sum-total bank represen- tation of the produced wealth into 180,000,000 bank accounts, each varying according to the individual's labor value, and turn each of the 180,000,000 bank patrons loose to write checks for those goods as they might require them or seek them. So long as they write no 'rubber' checks for more than each has in the bank, they may use up the exact bank credit that represents those produced goods.

"It is quite as simple as that.

"There is where the dividends 'come from' to pay the 108 million adults and the 72 million children! And no- where else!"

THE FOREGOING illustration taken from *No More Hunger* should impart to you the most basic funda- mentals about money. If you grasped it, you will no longer be misled or confused by harebrained economists who know the price of everything and the value of nothing.

The cardinal fundamental that should be indelibly un- derscored in your thinking is this: *Money, in any form, can only have true being and value as it directly reflects human effort.* It cannot have value of and by itself. It should not come into existence so that work can be done. It should automatically come into existence as work *is* done.

This is simply stating that "money," whether in the form of cash or checks, should at all times have a direct relationship both to goods produced and services rendered. Every "dollar" is merely an *earned claim* against goods and services available for purchase. It is a unit-measurement of some form of human effort.

At this point it should be readily apparent that we as a nation have permitted money to play just the opposite role. We have permitted ruthless financial strategists to set up institutions in our midst that have completely subverted the role of money as a unit of measure. They not only have usurped the power to create money, or credit, by the mere stroke of a pen but have made a "product" out of such fictitious wealth. Not only must the citizen, which includes the United States government itself, pay rent or interest for the use of such "paper" products, but, more seriously, he must compete against them with tangible property and honest hard labor.

It is the foregoing circumstance that has finally led to the financial sacking of an entire nation. But even the manipulated indebtedness should not be the most disturbing and infuriating aspect of the whole monetary system that has become a cancerous growth on the body politic. We as a nation have become financially subjugated to the point where we are denied the right to work and do those things that must be done, that can be done and for which we have all the ingredients.

This is the tragic stalemate that our nation has reached. And why? If we reply honestly, we will have to make the shameful admittance of having gotten into the stupid plight of having no measurement by which we can identify the value of production, distribution and rewarding. We have turned over all such measuring units to the banking fraternity and the public be damned!

WHAT DEGREE of intelligence can be attributed to the carpenter who says he can't build because he has run out of "inches?" What degree of intelligence could be attributed to the farmer who said he couldn't plant or harvest because he had run out of "bushels"? Is it not fair to ask what degree of intelligence does a nation possess which says it cannot put millions of men to work and start the wheels of idle machinery in order to produce things that the people sorely need because it has run out of "dollars"? What do *you* think?

Indeed, it is wishful thinking devoid of all logical reasoning to propound any remedies for the solving of our economic ills, which do not recognize as the first major reform the complete overhaul of our monetary structure. Sound and workable economics dictate that all forms of liens, mortgages, interest and fictitious debt-money be eradicated from the American economic arena.

Banking henceforth must become strictly a government function, serving only as a clearing-house for the claims of all citizens against their rightful share of all goods and services!

Only in such an environment can a nation grow materially with full utilization of its best scientific technology and guaranteed employment to every citizen who desires work. Only within such a framework can a real and dynamic meaning be given to *purchasing power*. Never again need economic growth be dependent on confiscatory taxes or the whim and caprice of those who control the nation's purse strings.

We don't need the "money" of the money-merchant or the international financier to conduct the nation's business.

We need only to unleash the fetters with which they have shackled us!

The Money Question Is Not New

The Colonies would gladly have borne the little tax on tea and other matters had it not been that England took away from the Colonies their money, which created unemployment and dissatisfaction.

---Benjamin Franklin

All the perplexities, and distress in America arise, not from defects in the Constitution or confederation, not from want of honor or virtue, so much as from downright ignorance of the nature of coin, credit and circulation.

--- President John Adams

I believe that banking institutions are more dangerous than standing armies. Already they have raised up a monied aristocracy that has set the Government in defiance. The issuing power should be taken from the banks and restored to the people to whom it properly belongs.

---President Thomas Jefferson

The youth who can solve the money question will do more for the world than all the professional soldiers of history.

---Henry Ford, Sr.

Permit me to issue and control the money of a nation, and I care not who makes its laws.

---Mayer Anselm Rothschild

~ 2 ~

Freedom cannot be Bought but Only Earned!

THE OTHER DAY a letter arrived in the mail that caused our blood pressure momentarily to rise several degrees. Its implications merit consideration. However, reference to it is not intended as any harsh indictment of the writer. Unfortunately, the feelings and conclusions expressed are characteristic of too many Americans.

The gist of the letter was simply this: "I have received a sample copy of your magazine. For many years we have read magazines telling of what's wrong and nothing has happened to solve our problems. You are just wasting your time. People haven't suffered enough. No, we are not interested in your publication!"

The initial reaction, was of course, to grab a sheet of paper, insert same in the nearest typewriter, and mince no words in accusing the writer of having succumbed to the nation's despoilers, of having spinelessly accepted defeat, and having let down shamefully the divine in man's action and makeup. But the impulse was short-lived. Sober reflection gives rise to the disturbing conviction that America contains tens of thousands of similarly pathetic citizens.

We do not refer here to those citizens who are blind to existing wrongs. We refer to those citizens who, to a large degree, are informed about the nation's ills but who accept that it is futile and hopeless to try to liberate themselves from the shackles that bind them, who feel that the forces holding sway over the majority are now too strongly entrenched to be ousted, and who fear dire consequences for those who openly champion the cause of honesty and fair play amongst all peoples.

Now it would be unfair to dismiss such misgivings and uncertainties with a wave of the hand. The vested enemies of mankind are powerful and it is indeed unrealistic to expect that they will relinquish their abnormal control until forced to do so. Also it is obvious that they are in a position to penalize those who will not conform and who advocate a more constructive method of conducting the affairs of the nation.

BUT WHAT has such a surface appraisal of the contest to do with a people's willingness to "throw in the towel" just because momentarily the opposition has bribed the referee, made his own rules and garnered all the gate receipts"? Should we not take note that his punches are weakening, that the odds are not all against us, that the victory can be ours if we display the will to fight to the last round?

The will to fight! This is our shortcoming. We have lost our dynamism to act in defense of our own birthright. It is not destroyed, but it must be reactivated. It must be aroused to a keener sensitivity to wrong and a more encompassing vision of the kind of America that awaits our enjoyment if we but gird up our loins and perform with conviction!

Make no mistake, that which is honest and wholesome and right will prevail in the ultimate denouement of event. We live and perform in a Universe that is good. Both balance and purpose underlie its conception and existence. Constructive, evolutionary change cannot be stayed by any force, however seemingly all-powerful it would appear at the moment. Make these cardinal points in your thinking and you will possess real ballast in confronting the stresses and strains of our turbulent times.

LET US consider two specific aspects of the currently existing conditions: First, the overwhelmingly unworkability of debt-money "capitalism," with its resultant and unchecked monopolistic control of the entire economy by the few while the majority becomes more and more dependent on bureaucratic government supported by unchecked taxation and indebtedness. Let us later consider the impact of technology, which uncannily is leading to the inevitable setting up of one large corporate structure, within which all the people's needs can be provided for in a secure and abundant life for each citizen.

Over the years a preponderant number of Americans have accepted that "capitalism" is synonymous with our most cherished ideals, that it is somehow the handiwork of our Founding Fathers, and that in a basic sense it embodies our inherent rights. This is sheer nonsense. In reality it is none of these. Equally serious is the mental-conditioning, which accepts that anyone who questions the workability of "capitalism" must be a Communist!

The foregoing misconceptions must be dispelled from our minds if we are to make any meaningful strides in working out our problems. This can best be done by understanding how "capitalism" was introduced into the American scene and of the economic theory that if all forces in society, labor, management and capital, are permitted to compete openly and freely to the maximum extent of their influence, the nation will enjoy the maximum materials benefits. Generally, this system is popularly identified as the "free enterprise" system.

THERE IS nothing sacred about the origin of "capitalism." There was no proviso for its inception in the Constitution. In fact, it did not truly come into full flower until the Industrial Revolution of 1848. This came with the introduction of powered machinery and the factory, the so-called "division of labor", into the economics of both Europe and the United States.

Instead of production being carried on by the individual, who performed all operations, the advent of power applied to machines made necessary group endeavor or a pooling of resources. In the majority of cases, it meant the need to "capitalize" the new enterprise with "capital" or borrowed money from banks or individual speculators, both foreign and domestic. For such underwriting the monied interests received owner ship of the controlling shares of the corporation or else they extracted their profit in the form of interest. If the enterprise was unsuccessful, then as now, the assets reverted to the moneylenders.

"Capital," the root of "capitalism," deals with the monetary and credit aspect of our whole economy. It is impossible to understand why it was inevitable that our economic structure would present insurmountable problems without grasping the ramifications of "credit" created and manipulated by privately owned institutions.

Conscienceless and ruthless interests began to entrench themselves in our midst almost simultaneously with the adoption of the Constitution. Their real takeover of the economy began with the Industrial Revolution, and with the passage of the infamous "Federal Reserve Act" in 1913 they gained their supreme triumph in obtaining a central banking structure that insured their complete dominance of the nation's whole bloodstream.

In the April issue of *The Eagle's Eye* we devoted space to this facet of our economy. There is, however, another facet that must be considered which falls under the much-lauded heading of "free enterprise."

It is simply splitting hairs to plead which designation is the most appropriate for labeling our economy. "Capitalism" and "free enterprise" are commonly used interchangeably. The more important consideration is that our economic structure is unworkable because its contains within itself the seeds of its own destruction.

E ARLIER in this article we mentioned that our whole economy is premised on the theory that if all forces in society are permitted to operate without any restraints, the general welfare of all people will be served. The theory goes all the way back to Adam Smith's book *The Wealth of Nations* in which was advanced the *laissez faire* or "hands-off" policy. Although this doctrine pertained primarily to non-intervention by government, it

31

became the underlying thinking respecting all forces in society and has held sway right up to the present moment.

It has become a bugbear in our economic thinking at a time when Twentieth Century technology screams for new approaches and new premises upon which to build a healthy and workable economy.

It would be fair to state that the economic history of this nation has been a gradual and systematic procedure of fewer and fewer interests being able to siphon of more and more of the wealth of the nation in both profits and assets to the final stultifying of the whole process. It has been the law of the jungle applied to a nation's economy. It is the principle of Might makes Right and makes a shameful mockery of the much-professed Golden Rule!

Any dispassionate review and analysis of our "free enterprise" and "capitalistic" system bears out that as the nation's productive ability increased through the science of mass production and the technology of automated machinery, the fallacy of the "profit" system became more and more evident.

Periodic panics and depressions, more popularly referred to as recessions during current times, are but the unavoidable periods when a manipulated shortage of purchasing power causes enforced unemployment because the people have been short-suited of their rightful claim against the abundance of goods they have produced!

THE safety valves that existed in the past no longer exist. In the past when the buying power of the people was insufficient to purchase all goods produced, the monopolistic owners of industry could start new industries with their accumulation of profits. Also there was new land to be exploited. Or limited wars could be brought about that bailed out the system with callous disregard to the needless spilling of innocent blood.

With the turn of the century, it could be said that the whole debt-money, capitalistic economy had turned the corner and was headed down a road that could only lead to collapse. It was but a matter of time. It was inevitable because it contained within itself the flaws whose effects must inescapably become more devastating and lasting.

Ironical indeed is the fact that it was to be man's flagrant misuse of his own advanced knowledge that would administer the *coup de grace* to a system of producing and distributing that made love of the dollar more important than love of man himself.

It has been the technology of automation, or the unlimited capacity to perform work with machines, that has accelerated the final corralling of the major assets of the nation into the hands of the few. No longer can shortage of purchasing power be substituted by further indebtedness and bureaucratic government spending through ever-increasing taxation.

The nation has all but reached the breaking point.

In the area of deteriorating international relations, or war, the possibility of making a blackened cinder of the whole planet is but fifteen minutes removed. Again, those in the past who could profit and increase their power through "controlled" wars, have misused science to threaten the extinction of all civilization.

Nuclear weaponry is indeed profitable, but even to the wicked and greedy its horrible potential for destruction must pose disquieting moments. It is no respecter of persons.

WHAT we have to get indelibly implanted in our thinking is that it is not technology or nuclear power as nuclear power that is wrong. It is the use to which it is applied.

For the same technology that has accelerated the taking of profits by the few and made millions jobless, if directed constructively, can provide for an abundant life for each and every citizen. The same nuclear power that supplies the terrifying explosive potential of nuclear warheads, which can level whole cities can, if employed constructively, furnish the harnessed energy to forever lift grueling and back-breaking labor from the backs of all mankind on this planet.

The biggest and most encompassing lesson that man must learn during this Twentieth Century is to employ his tools, his resources and his ingenuity so that they serve man. Any other course will mean his destruction!

The immediate lesson to be derived from existing conditions is that it is the system itself, by whatever name you label it, that does not permit constructive use of our know-how and tools. In a basic sense, it is not the development of *bigness* in production, with a few giant coordinated enterprises producing ninety percent of all goods and services, which is wrong. What is wrong is the fallacy of the "profit" motive that has pyramided the ownership of the nation's productive capacity into the hands of the few while at the same time denying the worker his rightful claim in wages against the goods he has produced.

Equally wrong is the fallacy of privately-owned institutions possessing the arbitrary power to manipulate the nation's credit without regard to any direct relationship of production to distribution,.

THE uncanny development of this century is that while the giant corporations have expanded through ruthless price-fixing and exorbitant profits, and have made a sham of competition, they have perfected coordination and efficiency in employing the latest technology. Even more important for our consideration is the fact that the *corporate* structure, successful for the few, gives us as an entire nation the pattern within which a truly abundant economy for all could be worked out.

It is in the cards for this to happen. The evolutionary process decrees its!

The moment, of course, someone advances the idea of a Cooperative Commonwealth, or corporate structure, for the conducting of the nation's entire business some well-conditioned victim will retort, "But that is *state ownership!*" And sixteen people within hearing will nod in their innocent stupidity. The tragedy is that they have been so brainwashed they have lost the ability to think for themselves.

Isn't it odd that it seems quite proper for a handful to own over ninety percent of all stock in the major corporations and it is wrong for all the citizens to own such stock? Isn't it the ownership by the handful that has caused the breakdown that is upon us? At the same time, isn't it the vast producers and consumers that in the larger sense make possible the building of any large productive enterprise?

It is sheer nonsense, devoid of constructive logic, to conclude that the corporate commonwealth provided for in *No More Hunger* is state ownership. What is proposed is *people's* ownership and directorship, which is a far cry from any form of arbitrary governmental control and dictation.

FOR the person who wrote Aquila and bemoaned the futility of trying to correct existing wrongs and eliminate the abnormal power of minority groups, let us hope that he will grasp the significance of portending event. The days of those wielding arbitrary control over the nation's vast productive machinery and those holding unentitled, unpayable liens against both the citizenry and government are numbered.

No system is workable or rational that deems man dispensable and ignores the needs of both his body and spirit!

The big role that has to be performed is the educating of the people respecting the alternative that awaits their endorsement. Little can be said for the timidity that makes people shirk from advocating those solutions that mean their liberation.

All we need is the will to act. No longer can we be insensitive to wrong. No longer can we refuse to play our part in rebuilding this nation.

People of like minds and hearts can create a dynamism of action that makes today's goals tomorrow's reality!

~ P ~

Seven Principles

IF I WERE at the head of this nation for a period, despite the seeming sentimentality of the utterance, these are the Seven Principles on which I would base my administration:

First---Have the forces under my control been administered this day so that love of humankind for one another has been enhanced in its broadest aspects?

Second---Have men learned anything from the functioning of government today that has privately ennobled them?

Third---Have men been taught to stand any straighter and firmer on their legs from what I have personally administered this day, and enticed by example of Great Public Office to look at each other fearlessly yet lovingly?

Fourth---Have men had any examples reared before them of compatibility in administration that will unconsciously motivate the smoother administration of their private lives?

Fifth---Have men seen anything in the future, motivated by Government, which enhances their prospects and belittles their failures?

Sixth---Have men known what it is to suffer today in experiences, not for other men's wraths or concupiscence, but for their souls' profit?

Seventh---Have men been so inspired by Government today that they are willing to die for one another, yet live for one another the more prosperously and beautifully?

Nations-in-law by William Dudley Pelley

~ 3 ~

A National Cooperative Commonwealth!

PERHAPS no misconception of thinking needs more clarification by the people before real strides can be made toward eliminating the nation's problems, than the idea that "rugged individualism" justifies the current dog-eat-dog system of economics. This misconception has been advanced and fostered by minorities who not only least appreciate the inherent rights of man but who are most guilty of restraining the individual in performing to the utmost of his individual potential.

Through deliberate propaganda the people have been led to believe that whereas it is quite in line with the concept of "free enterprise" for monied and industrial cartels to "cooperate," a better word would be "conspire," for the benefit of the few, any approach by the people themselves to work out their economic problems in a cooperative way smacks of some foreign ism, or is unworkable.

In other words, it is quite proper for a handful of power-hungry individuals to plan an economy to the detriment of a nation but it is wrong for the people as a whole to plan for their own equitable economy.

Mark this well: We as a nation live, struggle and endure under a planned economy so absolute in direction and control that it makes a hollow mockery of any suggestion of free competition. It is planned by the few at the expense of the many. Since when, then, is it wrong to plan a nation's economy, through intelligent cooperation so that it benefits 185,000,000 people?

UNDER a cooperative commonwealth, as provided for in *No More Hunger*, the first consideration would be that production of goods and availability of services be geared directly to the people's needs and highest desired standard of living. Such over-all production would be carried on within the framework of a national corporate structure with each share-holding citizen having a checking account claim against the total production according to his contribution in talent and work.

The total claims would be equal to the total goods and services, thus placing in the hands of *all* people a purchasing power that would buy *all* goods and services available.

It is not difficult to envision under the foregoing premise that the full utilization of productive capacity and technology would be made use of in carrying on production in the most efficient and practical manner. Bear in mind that we now have a blueprinted technology, or automation, which if used to fully benefit the people, would require only one-tenth of the total labor force, or 7,000,000 men to produce not only everything we use at home but everything we sell abroad.

What plea of intelligence can we make when such potential lies idle?

The second consideration would be that the whole, archaic, fictitious conglomeration of money and "credit," which has plagued mankind with its unhallowed and illegal functioning over the centuries, would be eliminated. Along with it would go all the evils of loans, interest and mortgages, all unnecessary liens against man's future. Henceforth, the Citizen's Banks, or clearing houses, would simply keep a running audit of each individual's checking account which along with all other accounts would be based on the only true value existing, total goods and services made possible by human effort.

Did you ever stop to realize that 95% of all transactions are now done by check, or by credit cards? An enlightened people would quickly bring to a halt the manipulations of the private banking structure, which has interlocked itself with the concentrated wealth of the industrial cartels.

No longer would a nation do business on "fountain pen" credit and exchange of currency, which have no intrinsic value but the willingness of an unsuspecting people to so consider them.

How would the worth of each individual be determined? Here we consider two basic points. First, under a constructively organized economy no one could have a claim against total goods and services beyond that which he could use, nor would there be compensation of any kind except that based on some form of human effort.

It is a fundamental of sound economics that anything in the way of goods and services accumulated beyond the individual's ability to enjoy is now withheld from being enjoyed by others. Only the voracious and those who seek possession of goods to wield unentitled influence over their fellowmen would object to this limitation.

Secondly, determination of individual worth would be *negotiated* by those employed in each segment of our society, including those in government who perform legitimate services. Elected representatives of each group would meet with the Commonwealth's Department of Economics, and on a basis of skill, number of workers, and all possible considerations, would negotiate relative claims and prorate the amount of work necessary to produce all goods and services for an abundant life for all.

There is no other way, or approach, to democratically determine worth. It is negotiation with a fair outcome to all.

In so brief an article, it is impossible only to set down a skeleton outline of how a nation's economy could be carried on to the maximum profit of all citizens. The complete availability of educational opportunities, medical underwriting for all citizens, etc. must be left to other articles.

If *you* do not possess a copy of *No More Hunger* by all means send for one so that you can have a more thorough grasp of how such cooperative commonwealth is workable, practical and attainable.

THERE are those who will entertain misgivings as to how such major adjustments in our entire economy could be realistically achieved under present owner-ship! Certainly the present owners are not going to relinquish their abnormal power and wealth!"

Frankly, it is astounding that so many fail to appre-ciate the irrefutable fact that absolute power, inher-ently and constantly rests with the people. It is within the rightful province and power of the people them-selves to make whatever adjustments or alterations as will more equitably and beneficially improve their con-dition. We should bear in mind that we function under a structure of government, under our Constitution, that provides for legal change whenever a majority of the people so deem it necessary and desirable.

Wisdom, of course, would dictate that change be made with the least upheaval and stress to anyone.

Foremost, we must recognize the undeniable fact that the concentration of our entire productive capacity in the hands of five percent of the population has come about through a premeditated defrauding of the Ameri-can people who make up the total of workers and con-sumers. The giant industrial cartel didn't come into being of and by themselves. They are the result of years of man-hours contributed by workers and man-agement. They have grown to their present size by expansion made possible by the exorbitant profits made from the sale of goods to the nation's consumers. It is now well established that 80% of all expansion of cor-porate cartels has been the result of the criminal practice of fixed prices.

Doesn't it seem strange that the only ones who ended up with equity and ownership of the giant productive cartels are a small handful of stockholders? Here lies the crux of the question as to who rightfully should own the productive machinery of a nation during an era of automation and bigness in production. No longer can an enlightened people forego their rightful equity and ownership to that which their human effort, represented by work and spending, made possible. It merits serious thinking.

The basic fundamental to bear in mind is that under any constructive economy only human effort, in either production or the multiple services, can command compensation. The current class of over-rich investors could not continue to derive their unearned profits. At the same time they would not be denied any rightful claim to which they were entitled under an adjusted economy. The small stockholder whose possession of stock represented invested earnings could have his legimate earnings returned to him in increased purchasing power over an allocated period of time.

To those monied and predatory interests that would shout, "Confiscation!" an insolvent and defrauded people must hurl the retort, "Too long have we permitted you to accumulate unearned profits taken from a productive capacity we built but from which we got a pittance!"

Automation and technology force us in this Twentieth Century to accept the efficiency and coordination possible in carrying on a nation's production by large-scale operations. This is the inescapable trend during this age of automated machinery and electronic computers.

There is no way of returning to an America of small, private, independent businesses to produce the people's needs. Progress will not permit it. We simply face the challenge of determining the control and direction of a productive capacity that can either further enslave man or liberate him to enjoy an economic and cultural existence beyond his most imaginative desires.

The prospect of a cooperative commonwealth is in the offing. Uncannily, the very structure and mechanics that have been employed to take advantage of the vast majority can be constructively used for their profit and enhancement.

It is an ill win indeed that blows nobody any good!

Our Beliefs

WE BELIEVE --- That Man is essentially and fundamentally good and his intellectual and spiritual enhancement is the motivating force underlying all human life in an Orderly and Purposeful Creation.

WE BELIEVE --- That such enhancement of Man is best served by the unlimited opportunity to investigate and to understand all human relationships and to comprehend the Universe to the maximum extent of his capacity for learning through a lifetime pursuit of knowledge.

WE BELIEVE --- That Man's inherent rights demand the full opportunity of developing and exercising his God-given talents to the utmost, and entitle him to his just share of nature's resources and the benefits of all human ingenuity.

WE BELIEVE --- That all government, all institutions of society, and all laws derive their powers solely from the people they are designed to serve and cease to have either authority or purpose when they fail to implement the constructive well being of all.

WE BELIEVE --- That Man's liberty to move, to express and to possess is in direct ratio to the same opportunity of all others similarly to perform.

WE BELIEVE --- That Man has an innate right to work out his destiny in an atmosphere of Peace.

~ 4 ~

Liberty is More Than Ringing of Bells!

No DATE in the history of this nation affords the American people such ample opportunity to display superficial patriotism as July 4th, the day on which the Declaration of Independence was adopted by the Continental Congress 187 years ago. This year was no different. In sheer sham and hypocrisy it has outdone all previous years.

As in the past the nation's civic groups and local governments made fervent pleas for all citizens to unfurl their flags. Tens of thousands bought new ones. Again the American Legion posts marched. Again the politicians extolled in most eloquent terms the virtues of the John Hancocks and the blessings we enjoy because of their undaunted heroisms. This year something new was added. . . .

At the stroke of one by the town clock there was a simultaneous ringing of bells across the breadth and length of this nation. Somehow this nationwide gesture was supposed to signify a nation's undying gratitude to those who affixed their signatures to the immortal document being commemorated. It was supposed to renew our love of freedom. It was supposed to re-dedicate us to a more vigorous presservation of our liberties.

THE CACOPHANY of bells tolling throughout America's cities did none of these. Why? Because it embodied no intrinsic meaning. It substituted emotion for understanding. It was out of step with reality, the hard cold facts of the society and the world we live in.

At best the whole gesture was a short-lived and ephemeral spasm of patriotic revelry!

Assuredly, a lot of well-meaning Americans were moved sincerely, even passionately. The Stars and Stripes and Liberty Bells have a way of making citizens stand erecter, bear themselves more proudly. We must differentiate, however, betweens symbols and life itself. The flag does not symbolize a freedom one whit greater than the freedom of the people who salute it. The Liberty Bell does not ring out our freedom one note higher than the freedom of the people who pause to listen.

We have become a nation of 185,000,000 people who are blind to reality. We hide behind the idealism and patriotic axioms of 1776 while we suffer conditions more intolerable than those that plagued the Colonists.

We have permitted high-falutin slogans and political jargon, devoid of practical meaning, to misdirect our minds from the real causes of our problems.

We have ceased to think clearly, candidly and analytically. Every American should read, and re-read the *Declaration of Independence*. It embodies every ingredient making for a free people. It dynamically presents the inherent rights of man, the purpose of government, and the perpetual right of man to alter or abolish that which does not implement and insure the people's well being.

Instead of all the flag-waving and discordant bell-ringing, how much more rational it would have been if at a designated time on July 4th a nation's sober attention had been directed to a reading and grasping of the fundamental guideposts on human relationships and social structures so clearly enunciated in the Declaration itself!

"We hold these truths to be self-evident: that all men are created equal; that they are endowed by their Creator with certain unalienable Rights; that among these are Life, Liberty and the Pursuit of Happiness; that to secure these rights, Governments are instituted among Men, deriving their just powers from the consent of the governed; that whenever any form of Government becomes destructive of these ends, it is the Right of the People to alter or abolish it, and to institute new Government, laying its foundation on such principles and organizing its powers in such form, as to them shall seem more likely to effect their Safety and Happiness. . . . "

Now it follows that a mere reading of the foregoing is not sufficient in itself. Few of our problems would be solved by so doing. The important achievement gained by focusing a nation's attention on the fundamental thinking of the Colonists would be that many people for the first time would grasp that it is the *people* who have the power, the responsibility and the *perpetual right* to solve their well being, to surmount every obstacle that restrains their inherent liberties.

First, however, the full import and impact of those problems and restraints must be understood. Unlike the Colonists who submitted a detailed list of the usurpations and abuses, which they were enduring, too many Americans of this day are oblivious to the even more severe injustices and needless suffering that permeates our entire society.

Only by fully understanding the nation's problems can commensurate solutions be forthcoming.

Life, Liberty and the Pursuit of Happiness! These are the goals of purposeful living. These are the yardsticks by which we should judge constructiveness of our government, the wholesomeness of our society. Such judgment should be premised on the over-all potential of our nation to provide abundantly for all its citizens. Any other premise is utter deception and dishonesty.

THE first responsibility of government is the presservation of Life. There is little reason to speak of other responsibilities if the paramount role of government is not fully served. What then of America's 32 million people (some sources set a higher figure) who are ill-fed, ill-clothed, and ill-housed? These are American citizens living within the boundaries of the richest country in the world on incomes less than $3,000 a year. Included in this number are 8,000,000 over sixty-five years old who have incomes less than $1,000 per annum.

Destitute, hungry, unable to pay medical bills, and with no opportunity to better their lot, these helpless millions are being denied the preservation of Life itself.

What then of between 5,000,000 to 6,000,000 Americans who are denied the right to work? In what way does government, or society, preserve life when anxious and able-modied men, with families to feed, clothe and educate, haven't a paycheck of a Friday night? Can we plead lack of tools, resources, or work to be done? Pray, what reason, what impulse do these distressed millions have for ringing liberty bells gustily on "Independence Day"?

The word liberty comes from the Latin word *liber,* meaning free. Webster's New Collegiate Dictionary defines the term as, "Exemption from slavery, bondage, imprisonment, or *control of another.*" In light of this definition, what realism, what practical, enjoyment of Liberty exists in a society within which economic monopolists, financial barons and political strategists are free to exercise abnormal power and *control* a bondaged and imprisoned majority!

Pursuit of Happiness! There are many definitions of Happiness and by no means should satisfaction with life be geared solely to the meeting of materialistic wants. There are several common denominators generally applicable to all.

Foremost would be that no man able and willing to work should be denied gainful employment. Such employment should be an individual's opportunity to work at the kind of job he enjoys, and should carry with it the equal opportunity for him to forge ahead and better his status based solely on talent and initiative. There should be no unearned incomes!

Pursuit of Happiness must mean real emphasis on the security and wholesomeness of the family unit. It must mean an end to broken-down tenements, dilapidated houses (one-third of the 58 million homes in America are *unsound* according to the 1960 Bureau of Census), and the complete erasure from the American Scene of the unhealthy and crime-ridden slum areas that belie any society's claim to being civilized.

Above all, for the whole vicious system of mortgages, interest and rent must be substituted a renovated arrangement of purchase so that every dollar goes toward direct ownership and it will be as unthinkable as it will be impossible to foreclose on or evict any family from its home.

NEXT, Pursuit of Happiness must mean the ability to have every medical aid that physical injury or illness would necessitate. No family can sleep restfully knowing that they are unable to meet medical bills if misfortunate should befall a member.

No society should enjoy a moment's peace of mind knowing that fellow humans right now are fighting a losing battle with death because they lack the pence to be under doctor's supervision and care!

In addition, Pursuit of Happiness means the opportunity to pursue knowledge to the maximum extent of one's ability to learn. By what logical reasoning should a child's right to full education be dependent on parental ability to pay the costs of his schooling? This is a prime obligation of any constructive society.

Real contentment, real satisfaction, real happiness would fill the hearts of every mother and father at the realization that their offspring, along with all others, were guaranteed the fullest, and equal, education for assuming their roles as the men and women of tomorrow.

Although these are the basic requirements of a people that seek sanity and purpose in their lives, they by no means convey the real achievement that would be possible. The real achievement would be the liberation of man from the duress of meeting material needs and desires to an appreciation and understanding of himself as a human being.

"Know thyself!" would become the criterion of meaningful living. All human relationships would rise above the greed and pettiness of status symbols. Desire to improve *oneself* and an appreciation of all other humans, in a good and understandable Universe, would underscore purposeful Pursuit of Happiness!

THERE are those who would say that we are uttering the vaporings of madmen, that we are picturing "pie in the sky," and some sort of Utopian dream. How shallow are such stereotyped parrotings by those who haven't devoted five minutes to analyzing our problems and have spent even less time in practically considering what a stupendous potential exists for building an Abundant America!

One thing is certain: Until the American people face up to the inescapable fact that their lives, their human effort, and their livelihood, are all, at this moment, shaped and manipulated by economic, financial and political power-blocks that function within *systems* that are one-sided and unjust, there can be no lessening of their suffering. There can be no justice or equitable enjoyment of our productive capacity until we install new methods by which a green go-sign is given to the full utilization of our exploding technology and we receive full purchasing power against that which we have produced.

Make it part of your thinking that suffering humanity is on the threshold of being liberated from a perpetual nose-to-the-grindstone existence. This is dictated not by any group or ideology, but by forces of evolutionary change greater than any human agency. Yet each one of us is an integral part of such force.

YES, it is an unalienable right of man to *alter* that which is destructive of man's enjoyment of *life, liberty and the pursuit of happiness.* This fundamental provision is the heart and core of the Constitution of the United States.

The Christian Commonwealth can be installed within the framework of such governmental structure. All that is necessary is the united will and "consent of the governed" for a more just arrangement in the affairs of men.

As for unfurling the flags and the ringing of bells, let's hasten the day when we can do both with meaning and understanding.

Remember, they can never symbolize anything greater and grander than the people who display and ring them!

~ 5 ~

The People's Will is Always Supreme!

NOTHING irritates us at Aquila more than to have someone give forth with the puerile statement, "Sure, things are bad, but there's nothing that the people can do about it." This is blasphemy to our ears and our impulse is to grab the jellyfish citizen by the nape of the neck and shake him within an inch of his life.

We know that it would be unrealistic to minimize the magnitude of the problems that confront the nation. We know too that the minority forces that dominate all phases of our society to profit at the expense of the majority are not going to relinquish their abnormal control until forced to do so. At the same time, we know that it is the people's failure to *recognize* and *exercise* their God-given rights that underlies all of their prolonged suffering.

It is not an unfair indictment to make against 185,000,000 Americans that it is they who have slept while the despoilers and usurpers ransacked and debauched their nation. It is they who have refused to listen to leaders with insight and courage who unmasked wrongdoing. It is they who have floundered in despair while in their own hands rested all the power necessary to effect their own liberation.

We at Aquila have pulled no punches, and never will, in indicting the forces entrenched in our society that are responsible for hunger and suffering in a nation that has the potential for overwhelming prosperity for all. No words are too strong in arraigning the culprits in our midst who are immune to the cries of hungry children so long as their coffers overflow with ill-gotten gains.

However, we are slightly burned up, or we should say intolerant, of a vast majority of people who refuse to recognize and exercise their own birthright. In the final analysis, whatever our own personal dereliction of duty, we must all assume the full responsibility for the problems and dilemmas that beset us. There is no one else upon whom can be placed the blame. It is we, the people, whom God entrusted with the power to work out our own salvation and happiness, or lack of it!

NOW there is little point in belaboring our failures to act and protect our own interests. But it is extremely important that we get a few cardinal points indelibly engraved in our thinking. When we do, we will feel an urge to administer a good left jab at the first person we encounter who supinely alibis that "there is nothing that the people can do about it."

In the September issue of this magazine, we used an isolated island to illustrate and accentuate man's inherent right to expend effort for the maximum physical comfort of himself and his family. As a family unit it was obvious that their enjoyment of the material things of life was in direct ratio to an exercise of their God-given right to work. Any decree, law or fiat from a distant island that the raw stock on that island didn't belong to him and his family to be fashioned into useful products would have met with righteous protest. The absurdity of someone's erecting a fence around any part of Nature's bountiful storehouse would have been brazenly apparent.

Utilizing our same isolated island, but populating it with twenty families, numbering all told a hundred inhabitants, let us consider man's equally adamant right to absolute sovereignty in making all laws and rules for the administration of the island's business. Is anyone so naïve as to conclude that these forty adults, allowing three children per family, must seek authority *outside* themselves in order to set up an operating structure?

Certainly not! Whereas they were born with the right to partake of the raw stock of Nature, they are even more unequivocally born with the right to propound and live under those rules that preserve and enhance the rights of each individual. It is their well-being, happiness and security that is sought. Who else, if not they has the right to be arbiter of their destiny?

Can you envision anyone of the forty adult islanders withdrawing from the group because he felt the group lacked authority in itself to work out its own human relationships? Wouldn't it be equally asinine for the group as a group to install a social structure that became more powerful than the people themselves who alone had made it possible? Can you imagine their erecting any island-government, or formulating any rules, not susceptible to change as circumstance and event dictated the wisdom of so doing?

To all these questions we would answer with an obvious "no." Yet, just how strongly and dynamically do we really get the impact of their fundamental implications/? How firmly do we believe in the supremacy of the people to modify, alter, change, and even erect an entirely new government if such majority action meant a more wholesome and democratic life for all?

We would contend that if only a reasonably large segment of our society truly understood the inherent right of the people to exercise absolute sovereignty our problems could be solved in a fortnight.

OF COURSE there is more to recognizing the fact that all rights, all powers, stem from the people themselves. There must be the will to exercise those powers collectively. There must be the intelligence to do it constructively.

First, let us quit complaining about our individual plights and the suffering and decay of the whole nation. Let us be about the business of correcting those wrongs and injustices that we have permitted to happen. Let us display the character, premised on God-given rights, that eradicates all crooks, all usurers and all exploiters of human misery.

Recently, I read an article by the fighting retired general, Edwin A. Walker, who minced no words in charging both political parties with being "crooked, traitorous and led by slapstick buffoons." At one point he asked, "Shall we continue to be Republicans and Democrats, or will we recognize that we are members of the All-American Party and elect no one but dedicated Americans?"

Dedicated Americans! In all solemnity and fairness, we ask General Walker, as we continue to ask all so-called Rightists, *dedicated to what?* And after you find you're dedicated Americans, how do you get them elected through the mechanics of existing political machines that you so rightly indict as being completely rigged and affording no freedom of choice?

We at Aquila find no personal fault with the General Walkers of this nation. We know that they are well-intentioned and courageous. At the same time, we know that mere patriotic exhortations and appeals to idealism solve no problems. There must be specifics.

Too long have a goodly number of Americans shouted themselves hoarse simply against general wrongdoing and injustice in our land. Too long have they simply dedicated themselves generally to fairplay, to liberty, and to justice. This at its best only indicates desired goals.

As intelligent men and women it is a false hope that expects that those who designed our predicament will set it aright. No crisis solves itself.

What the nation sorely needs are men who not only recognize that in the hands of the people rests the power to effect all changes but who understand *what those changes should be.* It is the *changes* that demand our dedication.

The changes that we are dedicated to economically we have spelled out in the major space of this magazine since we commenced its publication. For the remainder of this article, let us consider the specific changes, or safeguards, that must be made in order to establish true political security. Self-determination of people means, and can only mean, that the direct will of the people prevails at all times.

Under a Cooperative Commonwealth, the following specific innovations are provided for:

1. Elimination of all political parties.

2. Power of the people to remove or recall any officeholder.

3. Power of the people to pass directly all legislation.

LET US enlarge on these proposed remedies and consider their soundness and practicality. It will then become apparent how political skullduggery, sham elections and special-privilege legislation can be consigned to the morgue for belated burial. Thereafter the nation can "live in peace"!

Only the most naïve and self-deluded amongst us believe that the average voter has any effective voice in either the choice or election of candidates for high office. On the other hand, the vast majority of voters have come to accept the two-party political system as a "sacred cow" divinely brought into being. To question its weaknesses or unworkability is to question the handiwork of the Creator.

We who are dedicated to the literal changes that solve literal problems want none of such superstition and maudlin sentimentality, all promoted by those who want men to be political slaves. Political parties inevitably become owned, dominated and directed by a nation's monied and monopolistic forces. The end result is always the same. Elected representatives' first loyalty is to the *party* and not to the *people*.

Under a government, which is truly of the people, by the people, and for the people, there is no need for political parties since each candidate for office would be a candidate of the people. It would mean the end of political machines, which put the furtherance of their own nefarious interests ahead of the nation's welfare.

All qualified candidates should, and can, be presented to the voters via public media and especially TV. Contending office-seekers should appear together in open forum, or debate, and all such costs should be underwritten by government through its sovereign people. Political parties are obsolete and unnecessary. In the public interest they must be dispensed with.

ELECTION of people's candidates for office is only the first step. The power to elect must carry with it the power to recall any officeholder who breaks his contract with those who elected him. Under a Cooperative Commonwealth precluding all personal gain and fraud only the most conscientious men would seek office. The right of recall, nevertheless, should be an intrinsic part of any sovereign people's political structure.

Both the foregoing innovations, however, are exercise of only partial sovereignty. The most important renovation that must be made is that the people themselves must reserve the right to vote directly on all legislation, including all major decisions, which bear on the nation's business and policy. No longer can this power or right be delegated or entrusted to others. A people who really want to be free must reserve it to themselves.

Before transportation and communication were developed to the point they have been today, there were physical limitations that made the role of the people impossible of full exercise. For the first time in the history of this nation, the people can now have constant coverage of government in operation. Television, along with the encompassing advancement in electronic communications and data-processing systems, have revolutionized the people's ability to participate in all decision-making.

The Twentieth Century's basic approach to legislation must be that elected representatives shall perform the function of proposing all laws, after careful deliberation, but the people shall pass the final vote before they are enacted into the law of the land. This will mean true exercise of sovereignty. It will mean the end of political chicanery in high places.

There are those who will contend that the people are neither capable nor interested in directly administering their own government. To those critics we say, "How do you know when the people have never had the chance?" We hold to the premise that any people, however small or large, are only interested in any endeavor as long as they can be genuine participants.

What point is there in voting if your choice of candidates is limited to that of political oligarchies? What incentive is there to take an interest in the affairs of state when your voice is impotent and ineffectual? Why write your representative about pending legislation when he has already been overpowered or committed to the designs of multi-million dollar lobbyists?

AGAIN WE SAY, give the average American real voice in making the laws of his nation, and the administration of those laws, and he will evince a dynamic interest that cannot be quelled. At least he deserves the chance. Those to whom he has left the running of his country up to now have made a botched up job of it.

It is well that each of us re-read the Preamble to the Constitution of these United States and take note that it commences, *"We the people* of the United States, in order to form a more perfect union . . . " Strange, isn't it, that it doesn't say anything about Democrats or Republicans? It seems that such is what we are led to believe.

The first step forward in solving both our economic and political problems is to recognize to the innermost depths of both mind and soul that the people are supreme in power. If they suffer, they have no one to blame but themselves. If they want freedom, security, prosperity and happiness, this too can be man's lot in life. The decision rests with the people.

As mentioned earlier in this article, you can't be dedicated just to freedom and other idealistic goals. You must be dedicated to *changes* that make those goals a practical reality. Otherwise you are simply engaging in self-deception and illusions.

The whole purpose of the Aquila movement is not only to convince the people that within their hands rests the power of making any change for their betterment they deem necessary or desirable, but also to educate them as to the reforms that must be embraced. We solicit others to join with us that the job can that much faster be accomplished.

Don't lose sight of the fact that the people are the trustees of our own well-being and survival.

There are no stand-ins!

~ 6 ~

Friday's Pay Check Is An Inherent Right!

$\mathbf{P}$ICK up a daily paper, scan any current magazine, tune into radio or TV, and invariably your attention will be attracted to references to the "most basic issue" confronting the nation. And what is this most basic issue? It is conveyed by one four-letter, single-syllable word, *Jobs.*

Jobs! Employment! Gainful occupation! Call it what you will. Here is the criteria for measuring the security or insecurity, the meaning or lack of meaning in the lives of all the people in any society. Jobs determine work, work determines wages, and wages determine the ability to purchase the products and services of human effort. The prosperity or decay, the constructiveness or inequities of any society are in direct ratio to the extent man is permitted to exercise his right to work.

Before citing statistics that we might better grasp the magnitude of the tragic circumstance of millions unemployed when there is so much work undone, let us consider this *right to work* as an inherent right of every human being. In so doing we can penetrate through the bigness and complexities of current society and predicate solutions on bedrock fundamentals.

64

Now there is nothing mysterious or highly academic in defining "right to work." The word "work" simply implies performing or the act of doing. Slightly expanded, it means the expenditure of human effort. When we speak of man's inherent right to work, we are simply stating the inalienable right of every individual *to expend human effort to insure and enhance his own survival and well-being.*

GET IT indelibly ingrained in your thinking that this right to perform, this right to expend human effort, is a right that you are born with. It is not right that can be usurped and denied by government, or any social structure, irrespective of any acquiescence on your part. Inherent rights cannot be abrogated.

What then can be the limitations on the inherent right to work? Perhaps this can best be understood if we momentarily entertain a hypothetical situation. Let us suppose, for purposes of illustration, that you and your family awaken one morning to find yourselves the sole inhabitants of a small isolated island. No other humans occupy your new homeland.

Looking around, you see that nature has bountifully supplied your island with resources. There are straight and sturdy trees out of which a home can be built. Animals and fowl abound to supply food and garments. You note the soil is lush with fertility.

Having been conditioned in a society where it was "good business" to erect fences around natural resources, you are reluctant to just help yourself to the raw stock so amply in evidence. Perhaps you even make a survey of the island to assure yourself that somewhere tacked to a tree isn't a sign reading "Keep Off, Private Property!"

Finally it dawns on you that all such "property" belongs to a Beneficent Creator and is not the result of human effort. This is the raw stock of Nature. These are the crude ingredients out of which usable products can be refined. Only the refining is required of man, and such refining is the true meaning of work.

At this point I am sure you can envision that there could be no limitation on the standard of living you and your family enjoyed on your isolated island but your own unwillingness to put forth human effort. Projecting your thinking into the future, doesn't it just follow that as you and your family increase your knowledge (science) as to better ways of growing, harvesting and building, and improve your tools (technology), your survival potential and well-being would progressively increase and be enhanced?

Certainly you would have full enjoyment of the fruits of your labor with no one to deny you the right to have the full benefit of your productive capacity!

It IS not necessary to carry this very simple illustration further. Its purpose was to implant in your mind two fundamental tenets that must underlie all economic thinking. Grasp them, hold on to them, and your have the basic yardsticks with which to measure the colossal absurdity of *five million* men unemployed and *forty million* pauperized in the richest country in the world.

First, make it a part of your bedrock thinking that all natural resources are here through the endowment of a Divine Creator and no man or group of men have any rightful power to restrict the availability of those resources from use by all the people.

Secondly, get the impact of the wrongness of any system or arbitrary control that denies man the *right to work* in fashioning those resources into finished products in direct ratio to his willingness to expend human effort.

In light of the foregoing tenets we must conclude that any economic structure that does not provide a job for every single man who wants to work, and does not employ a nation's natural resources and technological tools for the maximum benefit of all the people, is both unjust and unworkable. And it should be corrected!

There can be only one goal for any constructive society, be it a hypothetical island-family or a nation of 180,-000,000 citizens, and that is full production and full employment.

Doesn't it seem strange to you, as it should to every American who gives it a moment of serious thought, that as we have doubled, tripled and multiplied manifold our ability to grow food and fibers, to extract resources from land and water, and to refine all raw stock into usable products through improved tools and knowledge, the security and well-being of each has lessened?

How could it come about that you should have lesser enjoyment of the fruits of your labor just because less human effort would be required? How could it come about that the greater ability to produce would mean less and less claim against the abundance produced and your eventual listing on the roster of unemployed? How has it come about that an entire nation has become beggared, insecure and hopelessly indebted in a land of superabundance?

These questions must be answered by each of us. They *can* be answered. In so doing, the solutions to our economic dilemmas are made apparent. All we need possess is our God-given common sense and the forthrightness to apply it.

The first major consideration or evaluation we must make is that capitalism as our economic structure does not *gear production to use, does not provide for rightful claims in purchasing power against production, and* does not *give each willing worker constant employment.*

Do we possess the candor and courage to face up to these basic flaws in capitalism? If not, we may as well throw up our hands in hopeless despair as far as liberating ourselves from drudgery, degradation and depravity is concerned. We deserve to suffer and should have the honesty to quit complaining.

CAPITALISM, as we have stated in previous issues, is not resources, tools and manpower. Those tangible ingredients are simply used *by* and *within* the system known as capitalism or by the misnomer of "free enterprise." This distinction is tremendously important.

Another way of expressing the distinction is to state that capitalism is a system of *owning, controlling, directing* and *profiting* from the employment of a nation's resources, tools and manpower. Or we might simply state that that such a system has brought about a circumstance where the few have been able to mercilessly exploit the many through denial of the individual

68

citizen's rightful claim to a nation's productive capacity.

Get it straight in your thinking that the economic structure we function under, more appropriately *slave* under, is a manipulated and planned economy. From stock ownership to calculated scarcity, from built-in obsolescence to conspiratorial price-fixing, all basic laws of economics have been violated. We have only been conditioned to believe it is a free economy. It is time that we awaken to this reality.

What are the two basic 'gimmicks" that make capitalism operative and exploitive? The first is the whole fallacious theory of "profit" as the only incentive to work and production. This propaganda has been the whole camouflage behind which monopolies have mushroomed into despotic enterprises through ruthless price-fixing and elimination of all competitors.

Profit as a charge extracted from the consumer, beyond any intrinsic worth of a product, is nothing short of legalized robbery. The monopolistic and arbitrary power to "administer prices" is a power *to tax* the people so that multi-billion dollar industrial empires can grow ever bigger, and controlled and owned by fewer and fewer property barons.

The other gimmick of capitalism is the whole complex of banking and credit by which private institutions (the Federal Reserve System) can create "unearned" dollars to compete against the "earned" dollars of the people. In the former case the banking fraternity creates claims against the nation's production and services by mere entries in its books. In the case of the people, they must put forth human effort (work) in order to exert any claim against that which has been produced.

Is it any wonder that the time would arrive when the Merry Game of extorting *unearned profits* and *unearned dollars* to the tune of hundreds of billions of dollars would reach a breaking point? The American people have been the unsuspecting victims of a gigantic gaming-device where the overwhelming odds rest with the Usurers and Profiteers. It has been a rigged game from the beginning. How much longer are we willing to prolong the game with chips purchased by claims against the earning power of future generations?

Every week over 30,000 jobs are lost because of automation or the displacement of men by machines. Each week over 26,000 new workers are entering the labor force. This means that over 3,000,000 new jobs must be supplied each year, or the unemployment list, now hovering around 5,000,000, will steadily climb unchecked. The outlook is very little short of disasterous!

A few months ago Secretary Hodges of the Commerce Department unabashedly admitted, "We are buffaloed!" John I. Snyder, Jr., president of U. S. Industries, Inc., a large maker of automatic equipment, stated, "We are not going to employ everybody here. Let's send them to places where they are needed." This callous remark was in support of a plan to export workers to Western Europe.

Neither honesty, nor even intellect, is evidenced in any solution advanced by those in high political office or the chief beneficiaries of the capitalist system. Long ago they learned that constructive criticism of the system is not to be tolerated. Political reprisals, economic pressures and character assassination await all who do not toe the line.

The most pathetic segment of our society are those who currently hide behind the false security of status symbols. They refuse to see the bold handwriting on the wall that calamity and bankruptcy face all if constructive change is not effected. Why should they worry if literally tens of millions suffer from lack of food? Momentarily, their families have enough to eat, their medical needs are met, and they are quite able to send their offspring to the best schools of higher learning. Secretly, however, they know that much, very much, is wrong with the nation.

But right now we are not overly concerned about the "haves" in the nation. Our heart goes out to the millions of victims of an economic and financial system that not openly has beggared them so they can't buy the bare necessities of life but has denied five to six million of them any Friday-night pay check with which to keep body and soul together. The magnitude and inhumanity of this injustice cannot go unchallenged.

WE NOW come back to the commencement of this article on the *right to work* as an inherent right. We endeavored to convey at the outset that man's enjoyment of life should be in direct ratio to his willingness to expend effort. The only limitation, other than his own unwillingness to work, would be a lack of raw stock out of which to make usable products.

It is in light of the foregoing premises that every person should be able to adjudge the over-all crime against all of the people. One doesn't have to have a comprehensive understanding of the universal abuses and strangling strictures of the privately owned banking octopus. One doesn't even have to have a working knowledge of the arbitrary, ruthless control of the handful of billion-dollar monopolies that dominate the economy.

All one has to have is the common sense to pose this question: If America has an abundance of natural resources, especially in light of the untapped oceans and the skill to produce synthetics, and has the tools with which to convert raw stock into an over-abundance of any and all products that humans can use, *what* influences, *what* prohibitions, *what* forces, *what* mysterious or hidden powers exist that prevent man from exercising his God-given right to work to simply produce those things that make for a better life for him and his family? One might put it more simply. What is the circumstance that doesn't allow man to expend effort for his own survival!?

The tragic irony of our times is that in the past when none of the modern tools of technology existed with which more than enough can be easily produced for everyone as now, the average family fared much better. At the turn of this century it was as unthinkable as it was absurd to tell the average American that he couldn't put forth his own effort on farm or in small shop to provide what his family needed. The unholy system of "planned scarcity" had not as yet reached its present despotic dimensions.

There is little question but that the death knell of capitalism has been sounded. It now behooves serious-minded people to consider the sound, workable alternative that must be adopted. The errors of the past

cannot be repeated.   Needless and poignant suffering
must be erased to stay erased!

SUCH an alternative to capitalism must provide for a
basic structure within which no person, or set of
persons, can chisel off or steal from the hard work of
others. Its cardinal premise must be that no man can
be denied the right to work and every paycheck must
be based on some form of human effort.

Recognizing that all industry and technology can only
come into being through the combined efforts of all
people, both as consumers and as workers, every solitary person is entitled to equity in the productive
capacity of the nation. Under such combined ownership, all production could be geared to the needs of the
people, with full utilization of our best tools. There
would be no displacement of men by machines but
simply shorter hours, all the while maintaining one
hundred percent employment.

Of course it would mean exit for the whole complex
monetary structure with all its fictitious credit and
ruinous interest. Instead there would be a clearing-
house to record all expended individual claims against
the totality of goods and services available. This would
not mean that banking personnel would be without
jobs. For the first time they could be recognized for
genuine service and not be unidentified cogs in the
wheels of legalized extortion.

A COOPERATIVE Commonwealth is the answer to
America's ills, both economic and political. How long
the American people are willing to suffer and endure
hardships before embracing its splendorful and work-

able features can only be conjectured. One thing is certain: Sooner or later they must, or perish. Why then wait?

In the spring of this year John L. Lewis, president of the United Mine Workers, was honorary guest at a luncheon in his behalf. We quote a few of his most persistent remarks.

"Unemployment has become the major problem facing America, far more important than trying to buy people to oppose Communism in 144 countries of the world.

"We have nearly six million unemployed. Chances for employment were never dimmer for these men. I am astonished at their patience. But as long as their patience is maintained, the more violent will be the explosion when they reach the limit of their endurance."

The more violent will be the explosion when *all* the people reach the limit of their endurance!

We at Aquila only hope and pray that when that limit is reached, a people can explode with as little damage as possible and recover with intelligent cooperation.

This last is the role we are determined to fulfill!

Join with us!

He who will not reason is a bigot; he who cannot is a fool; and he who dares not is a political slave!

~ 7 ~

Taming the Big "Monster" Automation!

Nearly ninety-five percent of all the articles appearing in newspapers and periodicals about "automation" are written in an atmosphere of fear and enshrouded in mystery. Or they are so highly technical of content that the average reader requires a course on electronics or advanced mathematics to comprehend what is conveyed.

Yet, fundamentally, there need be no difficulty to understand or appreciate what is encompassed by our technology now most frequently termed "automation."

Let us commence by considering the earliest cavemen of our history's most primitive civilization. Either by accident, or by caveman ingenuity, the most elementary mechanical device, the lever, was discovered. Simply by putting a pole over a rock it was discovered that a rock, one exceeding the caveman's own weight, could be moved.

The discovery undoubtedly was astounding and not a little perplexing. We can envision the caveman rushing in haste to his fellow-cavemen and making his scientific finding known.

We have no recorded history of the impact that the introduction of the lever made but it could easily have created some grave concern. The professional rock movers could justly have felt that their jobs were in jeopardy. Perhaps it called for an emergency meeting of the Caveman Council.

We in this more advanced and complex society have no difficulty in looking back to such primitive existence and seeing the ridiculousness of any contention that the newly discovered machine was anything but a blessing to caveman civilization. An easier means had been found to do work. A way had been found to multiply man's effort. In its most practical consideration, it meant less aching backs!

It is almost eerie to realize that the very definition we would apply in defining the lever of the caveman is equally appropriate and accurate in defining automation. Automation is nothing neither more nor less than our *achieved* effort in finding better ways to do work. It is *the sum-total of all scientific and technological progress in perfecting machines and systems to perform work.*

SINCE the word "automation" is a word coined in recent decades, many people erroneously accept it as some new discovery of and by itself. It is nothing of the sort. It is the end product of all the discoveries up the centuries. Without all foregoing developments of machines, automation would be impossible.

It isn't necessary for us to undertake a detailed history of all the developments of machines from the time of the caveman's crude lever to our current ability to hurl a man around the globe and bring him safely back to earth. We should, however, appreciate the major revolutions in using machines to perform work and more importantly we should have a working knowledge of what is meant by automation.

Let us consider briefly the major advancements in putting machines to work and we will better grasp what our current explosive technology encompasses and what a stupendous potential to do work we possess. In so doing we will better understand the irrationality with which we are permitting our machines and our know-how to enslave us instead of serve us.

The first industrial revolution witnessed the substitution of powered machines for hand tools. This was the period when both steam and waterpower came into being and the small independent shops became factories. It all culminated in what every schoolchild knows as the Industrial Revolution. Instead of individual effort in making products, the whole concept of producing became one of group endeavor. Division of labor became the structural layout of every factory and the individual's effort was multiplied many fold through use of machines and production organization.

PARENTHETICALLY it might be inserted that at this point in our history had the nation adhered to sound economic principles, and had all parties involved only sought the maximum well being of all peoples, America could have set out on a road to prosperity and such achievement that neither hardships nor depressions could have visited this land. Not only was there an abundance of natural resources but one machine could do the work of many men. Power had been harnessed to do work. The lot of man should have progressively become easier.

Right here came into being the whole concept of capitalism in the financing, building and controlling of industry. Its inherent flaws and injustices were not to be quickly detected for the country was comparatively new, there was much virgin territory, and the pioneering spirit prevailed that ever led men to move out of "depressed areas" to start anew. The wrongs of capitalism were at first well camouflaged.

When the individual shoemaker made the completed shoe himself, he knew the effort he had expended and was in a position to protect his own interests when he traded or sold his shoes. However, when he went to work at the shoe factory and now performed only one operation on the shoe and received wages for his day's work, he was at the mercy of the factory owner. Being relieved of the responsibilities of running his own business, it did not occur to him that he was not getting his rightful benefit from machine production, and further that he was not realizing any equity or ownership of that which he was building in the way of an expanding industry.

Periodically, as is the case now, the result was an inevitable shortage of buying power. Goods piled up and factories closed. How could workers buy the goods produced if their wages fell far short of that which they had produced? But then as now they accepted that the amount they had been short suited was the rightful "profit" of the owners who simply set up new factories and the same cycle was reenacted. History refers to them as panics.

But this was only half of the picture. The profit-motive, artificial gluts and subsequent expanding ownership must be coupled with private banking in order to understand the over-all working of capitalism, or what today is unabashedly termed "free enterprise." Into the picture now came the money-merchants with the criminal, but legalized, power to create debt-money and fictitious credit.

Capitalizing of industry could be done by "fountain pen" credit and of course the worker was always a welcome patron of the loan companies just as he is today. If the loan wasn't repaid, the bank or loan company extracted its pound of flesh and, anyway, interest was duly collected.

Condensed to its basic essence America had two dollars. One was represented by work and was an *earned* dollar. The other was created and was an *unearned* dollar. It is the same today.

The foregoing is far too simplified and is set down only to show the methods of capitalism, the major flaws of the system, that have compounded over the years into the injustices and economic madness that is our plight up here in the 1960's. Isn't it strange that the vast majority of people haven't long ago recognized that they as both workers and consumers, together with management, have made the whole industrial structure possible, and therefore should have equity? We'll have more to say about this later. Right now let's consider the next large stride in industry.

WITH the turn into the 20th century we entered what might be termed the second industrial revolution. This was the introduction of the assembly line and the science of mass production. Whereas the application of power to machines doubled and quadrupled a single man's output, the division of labor finesse and organization of the assembly line increased the output per man-hour many, many times.

This was, of course, the era of applying the more efficient power of gas and electricity to the operating of machines, and the refining of materials as the raw stock from which to make finished goods.

No one in his senses can refuse to marvel at the tremendous strides that this century has made in new discoveries and the advancements made in transportation, communication and methods of production. These years witnessed the invention and mass production of the automobile, the innovation of both radio and television, availability of refrigeration, the perfection of air transport from the plane of the Wright Brothers to the stratoliner, the wide field of a hundred and one electrical appliances, just to highlight the past decade.

In place of the 100-man factory grew the giant corporations that employed hundreds of thousands. Products came rolling off the assembly lines in an abundance of varieties of necessities and luxuries. Our whole productive mechanism, or economy, became identified as an age of skilled men operating skilled machines. Millions of men were no longer needed to perform work and became numbered in the unemployed

The inescapable flaws of our system became more evident to those who were not afraid to face reality. They recognized that the progress the nation had made technologically had nothing to do with the system as a system. Such progress had been made in spite of it.

HOWEVER, a third industrial revolution was to take place that would make a mockery of any claim that our economic system was either sound or workable. Even to a greater extent than in the past goods would pile up, men would be made idle, and want and deprivation would stalk the land. Instead of panics and depressions, we would have the term recession.

This is the revolution of machines replacing man called automation. It had its inception in the 1940's but now in the 1980's gives evidence of a progressive impact that will be felt for the balance of this century in working out human relationships in producing and distributing to meet all the needs of all the people.

Earlier we referred to the age of mechanization, and the subsequent era of the assembly line, as *skilled men* operating *skilled machines.* Automation might be termed as an era of *skilled machines* operating *skilled machines.* Or it might be stated that electronic devices have been developed and perfected that coordinate and integrate all machine operations without the need of men to check or supervise the machine's performance.

The first introduction of automation was in the automotive industry and was called "Detroit Automation." This was the transfer machine, which simply made possible the coupling of a series of machines into a single line of production so that successive operations were automatic and could be supervised from a central control system. No longer was it necessary for skilled men to operate and supervise independent machines.

There is not an industry that has not been affected by this type of factory automation. Millions of men have been displaced by such automated machinery. The steel industry, the textile, the coal, the electrical field, the automotive, have had their work forces cut nearly in half, yet their productivity has risen in most cases over fifty percent. The story has always been the same, more products and fewer men to produce them. Without wages the millions unemployed have had to turn to government assistance, welfare, and indebtedness.

But wholesale displacement of production, or factory, workers is only half the picture of automation. With the introduction of electronic computers, the amazing machine systems that have unlimited capability to store and process data, we have machines that supplant large areas of man's thinking and decision-making.

The scope to which computers and data-communications systems can be employed are endless in application. Some computers have a capacity for making 250,000 computations a second. It is possible to store all the books of the world in one central system of computers and communicate instantly any desired knowledge to any part of the nation. Hundreds of thousands of clerical and supervising personnel have been replaced by computer installations.

And we have just scratched the surface of their use and application.

A THIRD TOOL of automation must be mentioned. This is what is called servo-mechanisms, which in conjunction with data-processing systems have not only made possible guided missiles but also all space exploration. The function of servo-mechanisms is simply to *automatically* correct errors and deviations in performance so that a mechanism will continue to function in a predetermined manner. More and more industries are employing servo-mechanisms.

This is just a brief coverage of the tools of automation. Limited space does not permit much detail about their functioning or application. Nor can we go into the hundreds of thousands of displacements of workers in all areas of our economy. Newspapers are loaded with statistics of ever-increasing unemployment and perfected processes of automation.

Suffice it to state that 40,000 *each week* are being displaced by automation and that 30,000 new workers are entering the labor force *each week* looking for jobs that don't exist!

What concerns us is not the statistics. What concerns us is human beings who in the accumulate made our entire technology and productive capacity possible but are flagrantly denied the benefit from that capability which can produce an abundance of both goods and services. We are concerned over the insanity with which manpower, our resources and our know-how are wasted while widespread deprivation and want affects tens of millions of our citizens.

THE most knowledgeable men in the automation field have testified that if we used our best technological know-how, which has been already blueprinted, it would only take ten percent of our entire labor force to produce both what we use as a nation and what we export abroad. This would mean only 7,000,000 workers employed. On this basis 63,000,000 men could be replaced by automation.

Obviously, this could only lead to open rebellion and mass onslaught on over-burdened warehouses. The five percent that own ninety-five percent of the shares of all industrial enterprises have no thought of permitting this to happen.

From their avaricious standpoint, it is better to permit machines to stand idle, delay application of our best technological engineering, and keep the system alive by ever-increasing transfusions of taxes and indebtedness, both public and private. Inevitably, there will be a breaking point.

Intelligent men and women cannot, however, merely await the inevitable. They must recognize that not only have the people in the nation been greatly wronged, but that these same people have the power in their own hands to make such changes in our economic structure as will permit one hundred percent employment and the maximum enjoyment from full utilization of our productive machinery. The power to act is theirs.

The uncanny thing is that the transition from a nation, hamstrung and burdened, to a nation, free and prosperous, can be executed without too drastic changes!

THE FIRST consideration must be that there is nothing sinister or wrong with automation as the most efficient way in which to produce all necessities. Nor is there anything sinister or wrong with the bigness of enterprise as such. On the other hand, we must face up to the inescapable fact that capitalism as a system of owning, controlling, and directing such tools and bigness is both sinister and wrong.

An enlightened people must positively announce, we have no objection to the corporate structure as a structure. It can be a democratic framework within which to conduct the nation's production facilely and efficiently. We contend only that the 5% of the families of America who own 95% of all major corporations did not *earn* such overwhelming ownership by *valid* effort. Conversely, we contend that in the final analysis all technological advancement, and the over-all capability of our productive potential, have been made possible by the *totality* of people, whether as actual workers, including management, or as buyers of the products and services of all machines.

We contend that it is the people's valid right to incorporate our entire economy into one nationwide corporation within which our whole productive capacity is employed, where all citizens are common shareholders by virtue of citizenship. This does not mean that a gradient scale of reward for initiative and merit should not be negotiated among all groups in determining relative contribution in keeping the over-all productive machinery operative. It does mean that human effort, not inherited or finagled ownership, should determine compensation.

Under such national incorporation, each common share would not only guarantee voting rights in the corporation, but would guarantee the basic necessities of life so that no individual in America could be forced to endure poverty. It would mark an end of all welfare, charity and dependence on relatives and friends to keep body and soul together.

Both government and private research defines poverty as having to live on an annual income under $4,000, for multiple-person families, and $2,000, for unattached individuals. They further bear out that one-fifth of the nation, or 38 million Americans, fall in this deplorable state. In light of our almost incomprehensible ability to produce, the stated minimum guaranteed sustenance for all our citizens must be the first right of citizenship and thus forever erase poverty from our land.

Preferred or merit shares would be issued to all who actively engaged themselves in working for the corporation. Such shares would command dividends, which would be the real wages of all citizens thus employed. It requires no wild stretching of the imagination to realize that a corporate economy, utilizing all the technology of automation, could produce such abundance that preferred dividends, plus the basic sustenance amount, would give the average worker a minimum purchasing power of at least $10,000 to support his family. Others would command much more.

IN ADDITION to the foregoing two kinds of shares, the corporation would issue Realty Shares to insure inviolate ownership of home. It could not be foreclosed on and every payment would be toward ownership. For the first time real security of home would exist in which to raise and counsel growing children.

Such a corporate structure would for the first time treat our elder citizens with the respect and dignity to which they are entitled, It would simply recognize that the aged have a real claim against the productive potential created. They helped to make it possible and should therefore receive continuing benefit. There is no reason in the world why citizens could not retire at the age of fifty and from then on enjoy life on incomes commensurate with that which they were enjoying at the time of retirement.

They would not be recipients of charity, nor would they need to be considered as dependents. They would already have earned by contribution of past effort the right to enjoy current benefits.

The acceptance of two major contentions is necessary to install the Corporate Commonwealth. First, that the productive capacity of the nation belongs to all the people who made it possible. Second, that henceforth only some form of human effort can command compensation.

Are there sufficient people who are willing to support these contentions in making a new and prosperous and constructive America a reality?

~ 8 ~

America's Youth
Voice of the Nation's Conscience!

HISTORY bares out that up to this present day there has not existed any group sufficient in numbers or strength to challenge effectively the inequities of predatory private capitalism. The very nature of a private capitalistic economy is the progressive weakening of the majority, making the people more and more dependent for their survival on the dictates of burgeoning power structures.

Militant groups, particularly in farming and labor, have arisen but have waged a losing battle. Their strength and numbers have dwindled in direct ratio to the advancements of technology with both farmer and industrial worker becoming dispensable elements in the economy. In the current economic quandary of unmet needs at the same time that there is unused productive capacity, society divides itself broadly into three somewhat overlapping segments.

At the bottom are the very poorest, those most justified in their plea for justice. Not only are they victims of false economic concepts, but as always they lack money, education and self-leadership. Unjustly they are condemned for their proneness to violence when in desperation or frustration they steal or kill or riot in order to acquire that which is denied them.

In the second segment we have the "backbone" of A-merica, which we call the middle class. Regrettably, this, by far the largest group, is least disposed to social change. Here we find the most ardent apologists for private capitalism. They are blinded by their own false sense of security, which they judge chiefly by the poverty of so many millions below them, and are so involved in the worship of "status" that they want no major change in the current system. However, pressures of confiscatory taxes and wastrel bureaucratic fiats from Washington are causing them considerable uneasiness.

In the third segment we have the power structures and the Establishments. Here we have all those tied into all the aspects of amassing holdings and monopolistic policy-making. We deal here with vampiristic private banking, the whole complex of industrial and military oligarchies, and the machinations of the major political parties. Those in the top echelons assume no moral responsibility for the well-being of the people or the nation, except through their own controlled "charities," and have arrogantly accepted that the sheer ability to subjugate and exploit human beings justifies in itself all such disservice. They have no disposition, naturally, to relinquish their usurped power and only an increasingly unsafe society is making them take note that their own unhallowed positions are in jeopardy.

Whence then comes the leadership and political strength for a renovated America?

First, an expanding intellectual leadership has arisen that not only recognizes the unworkability of private capitalism but sees the feasibility of alternative reme-

89

dies. In growing numbers they are coming to see that some form of a Corporate Commonwealth must be adopted so that the people not only will have *legal equity* in the nation's entire productive potential, thus assuring them of a constitutionally guaranteed purchasing power to buy all the nation can produce, but they must also have a *decision-making* voice in the directing of the nation's productive potential so that they will be the prime arbiters in determining their own well-being and in shaping their own future.

Secondly, almost overnight a force has emerged that in numbers, dynamism and political strength has the potential to bring about all constructive change. Such force is to be found on the campuses of this nation.

For years it has lain dormant because its members were primarily interested in becoming "trained" to fill the highest positions in industry and business or in the professions and government. They were generally the offspring of the wealthier who went to college as a matter of course and were oriented to the thinking of the "successful."

Gradually, commencing with the GI Bill after WWII, the college student bodies became interspersed with those coming from all strata of society. Opportunities to go to college increased greatly with scholarships, government loans, grants and the recognition that a high school diploma alone no longer insured employment.

The Civil Rights movement entered the scene to jolt the conscience of the young people that there was an idealistic America and there was an America that betrayed and belied our oftvoiced idealism. At the same time, the hidden America of the poor and destitute came into focus. Together, these two submerged blights of the nation awakened the conscience of the young on the campuses. Adult America, too deadened in spirit, awakened only statistically. The young's response was different. They responded in spirit, a communion of human beings, interested and concerned with their fellowmen who were in need of help.

While the adults may be motivated to assume a degree of *responsibility* for the less fortunate, only the young have the finer attribute of *respondability*. It is the quality of empathy, the ability to place oneself in the shoes and the consciousness of one's brother and endure and feel all that he endures and feels. It is sensitivity to wrong and a reverence for life itself.

Leadership cannot be true leadership without this quality. How can there be a qualification to speak for the poor and the disadvantaged in society if the voice does not come from their conscience? It is only the uninhibited and unshackled souls of the young who can respond freely to that conscience.

Even misdirected rebellion or protest is better than apathy and no conscience at all!

The young men and women on American campuses are the one group in the nation large enough to encompass the whole society in seeking total renovation. They are the only economic and political force in numbers who could furnish the strength and enthusiasm to overcome the force that persists in the status quo.

They are the only force that is uncommitted to any group and which is not yet molded into the system and vulnerable to intimidation and penalty. They reflect every strata of American life and they have training in the arts of communication.

The soul of America is beginning to speak with a new voice. It falls to the young to give it articulation, vitality and strength. After all, it is *their* America, and that of *their* children, that they are shaping!

~ 9 ~

No More Hunger

Bridge to a New Tomorrow

By Dwight B. Miller

LESS than a year ago, I discovered a book, written 33 years earlier, that not only presents positive remedies for our many ills of the present, but holds out an open promise for building our future. It demanded that I take action.

Why? For the first time, I saw charted a course of sanity and positive action, rather than absurdity and mere reaction.

The book is entitled *No More Hunger*. In its 208 pages I saw a practical way (and here I mean a possible, usable and feasible way) of eliminating such pure suffering as hunger, privation and soul-deadening "welfare," blended with a recognition of the vast scale of individual human differences and a plan for compensating each grade in the equally vast scale of individual accomplishments and contributions.

This book called *No More Hunger* is not just another anesthetic treatise on economics, filled with laws, charts, graphs, axioms, and the typical dead prose of men groping for answers in the guise of positive statements.

It is economics built on simple truths!

It takes into full consideration that our real wealth is no more and no less than our natural resources plus the sum of our *individual* accomplishments. Any wealth claimed beyond that is a myth, a fraud exposed and cancelled by the predictably rhythmic onslaught of panic, recession or depression.

It is built on the premise that the strength and progress of our nation can be no greater than the strength and progress of our least citizen. It is founded on individual productivity and prescribes in rock logic how we can develop the *incentive* necessary for just that, individual productivity.

Build the man. Give him not only the right but the freedom and encouragement to increase his self-awareness and self-expansion. *And we all gain.*

As the other man works, he helps himself. But he also helps me. How else would I now be enjoying the fruits of such as the Fords and the Newtons, the Kennedys and the Lincolns, the Salks and the Pasteurs, the Wyeths and the da Vincis, the Russells and the Platos, of all those who have cut paths that I can follow up the uncharted mountains of human effort, of all those who have had to fight incredible restraint in order to achieve?

No More Hunger, what it set down in 1933, shows me clearly that only as the other man works, and is encouraged to work, to his fullest capacity, can I hope to gain beyond the limits of my own puny abilities. By "work" here is meant not toil or drudgery, but any kind of constructive service or creative activity.

When all are thus productive, we all gain immeasurably. When one is forced to be idle, we all stand to lose.

Only when each man is assured of at least a minimum of food, of shelter and of clothing, free from the uncharitable debasement of "charity," only then can we be assured that he will begin to develop his capacities of productivity and achievement, for his own benefit and for ours.

These are the truths I found in *No More Hunger.*

Even more impressive than this clear picture of our real wealth is the disarmingly simple plan for putting this wealth into use. It can be achieved by the mere legal changing of our whole nation into the corporate structure.

Look about you. Check your daily life. Where can you turn that you do not find yourself under the influence, perhaps control, of corporations? Businesses, to be sure, effectively use the corporate structure to their definite profit. So do schools, churches, charitable societies, museums, even our government using the structure of corporations with its organization chart, the chain of command, and the delegation of authority and responsibility.

It is no stretch of logic to view all the business and industry in our land as one Giant Corporation, and operate with an annual profit or loss. So, if corporations exists about us in effect, why not make it exist in legal fact, and make our national economy work more efficiently?

It could all be achieved within the framework of the Constitution. It can, and must, be done without violence or coercion in any form.

We would be the United States of America, Inc. Each citizen, at birth or naturalization, would be a voting shareholder, a common shareholder. Each common share would provide a minimum of food, of clothing and of shelter, not as a dole, but as a birthright. Individual achievement would be compensated, with fairness beyond anything demonstrated on the scrolls of this earth's history, by preferred shares.

Nothing would change but the sham of our current techniques. It would be capitalism without fraud, without the massively self-leveling, individually destructive process of business cycles that mark the shabby course of our economic history.

But where do we get the money?

From the same source we get it now. From our resources and our abilities and our proven earning power, for these truly are the basis of the debt-financing that causes our suffering of today. These are what we put up as collateral for the credit so "generously" given us by the banks of today.

Look at this fact clearly. Our banks do *not* lend us something they have! They lend us something we already *had* before we ever entered their doors, our resources and our abilities and our proven earning power. They take what we already have, create a credit account in our name, based on nothing more than what we already possessed as we walked through their doors, then demand a lien on our future and charge us dearly for the "favor."

By this very process they have concentrated the wealth in the hands of a few (the current estimate is something like more than 95 percent of the wealth is in the hands of less than 5 percent of our people). Concentrated wealth is concentrated power. Fewer than 9,000,000 control what the other 181,000,000 do!

An incorporated America would eliminate such usury, such actual theft, and such destructive accumulation, not as a Robin Hood venture of stealing from the rich and giving to the poor, but in true equity and in fairness to all. It would make money exactly what it is supposed to be, a symbol of exchange instead of a commodity, a thing having no value unto itself. Nothing of real worth would change.

Our needs and our wants would still exist. Our hopes and aspirations would still be with us. Nothing would change but the odds favoring the fulfilling of our hopes and aspirations, our needs and our wants. Even today, with our wheels turning inefficiently, at a rate far lower than full capacity, we can glut the market, any market. We have the computer capacity to run a national warehouse inventory in a matter of hours, a communications ability to process all necessary orders in a matter of seconds.

We have the capacity, in resources and ability, to saturate every home, every citizen with the things that are wanted, needed and deserved. The question we must ask is, why do we *not* do this thing?

One answer that makes itself appallingly clear is that we have turned our attention too much away from the problems that plague our land. We have, in the manner of a slowly strangling octopus, assumed the role of "policeman of the world," an incredible position for a nation, not only founded on the principle of "self-determination of peoples," but which visibly cannot "police" the land within its own borders.

We do not see that force, like greed, is a self-defeating absurdity, that is an abomination whether in Viet Nam or in the Middle East. We cannot see from the clear evidence of all our written history that force breeds nothing but counter-force, hate nothing but counter-war, hypocrisy nothing but distrust and contempt. We do not yet see that only peace and prosperity can yield peace and prosperity.

We are trying to become the leading influence in the world today, by force. We fail to see that only as we perfect the premises set up in our document of origin, the Constitution, can we hope to become that very influence by example.

If we would lead, then let us lead in peace, clear, bright peace, and honesty. Let us set our house in order. Let us be as the Christ, a shepherd, not a drover.

Let us do that which is fully within our powers, make ourselves a credit to ourselves, a credit to all of us as a nation and a promise held out for the other citizens of the world. This must begin with economics, for no man can manifest in spirit if he is held in bondage through the purse.

As a nation, we must see these truths! To the extent we are productive, to that extent are we wealthy. To the extent that we stand idle, in body or in mind, to that extent are we poor. And to the extent that we perpetuate a system that results in periodic idleness, to that extent are we stupid.

We can make major change easily. All we need is people and the logic set forth in *No More Hunger*. If you think I speak balderdash, read it for yourself.

Because we can make this change, because we can better our lot, we must do so. The time to start is now.

Perhaps you believe that this is the kind of job that will be accomplished by a bolt of lightning, or by superior beings from planets afar. Personally, I think such miracles, particularly the latter, are unnecessary. There are millions of superior, two-legged mortals walking everywhere on earth, if they are given the chance to function.

It is truly said that God has but one effective instrument for change on earth. That is Man. There is nothing that cannot be accomplished if men choose to work together. The first step is to familiarize ourselves with the magnificent and workable blueprint for a better society set forth in *No More Hunger*.

We may then move forward to fruitful discussion and constructive action toward the better life for us all!

~ 10 ~

"What shall it profit a man, if he shall gain the whole world, and lose his own soul?"

Two THOUSAND years ago, a Great Teacher appeared on this earth. Dressed in the simplest of garments, He trod from community to community addressing all those who would listen to His preachments. He displayed no flamboyancy or oratory nor did He comport Himself as a demagogue seeking office. There were no frantic exhortations to "seek and destroy" the enemy, or beseechments to build bigger and better weapons to annihilate those with whom there was disagreement. His was a mission of love, an appeal to the hearts and the minds of men that the brotherhood of man was attainable if mutual respect underscored all human relationships.

And what did such mutual respect embody? Just two simple, but profound precepts: 1) Love they God with all thy might, and 2) Treat all others the way that you want to be treated. In two short sentences had been enunciated the cardinal guidelines for all constructive and interrelated human conduct. The scope of their application was limitless. How people lived together, the fairness of the social structure and institutions set

100

up, and the integrity of government that supervised all laws, were encompassed by these two plain and simple precepts.

This article is not meant to be a sermon. We do not intend to preach in favor of any particular religion. We are appealing here only to basic common sense. The world, and particularly our own nation, is in the throes of such aimless confusion and apathy, such vicious antagonism and violence, that failure to reverse the suicidal course we are pursuing can only end in mankind's destruction. Only a soul-searching affirmation of true values can restore ballast to our thinking and provide rational direction to a world engulfed in violence and wanton waste of energies. There must come into play a resurgence of reason, justice, probity, and reverence for all life.

These, however, can only be engendered by an unshakable belief in the basic goodness of man himself and in the acceptance that we inhabit a good and purposeful Universe. This is the message that the Man of Galilee tried so hard to impart to all of mankind.

What did He mean by, "Love thy God with all thy might"? Was He asking us to love some sublimated Moses perched atop some celestial pedestal who ultimately would pass judgment on the fallibilities of his own creations? This is the interpretation that has been given us by little minds. Is it not fairer to conclude that Jesus was pleading for man to have love and reverence for *all* creation? The beseechment to "love with all thy might" implies a full encompassment of all that surrounds man in countless forms of living and inorganic structures. More than that, it implies an impartial universe within which each human life has equal opportunity to shape its destiny and its well-being. What other justification would there be for "God" to merit the all-out love of everyone of His creation?

In more practical terms, we are simply recognizing the fact that this planet that we occupy, so abundant in resources and levels of energy, is the heritage of every human being born upon it. It is man who has depart-mentalized it and through greed and deceit fashioned a world of "haves" and "have-nots." It is man who has set up the rules, which have subjugated and impoverished tens of millions while the shrewd and cunning feasted at banquets. It has been man in his obsession for the spoils of war that has pitted one mass of innocent people against another so that economic or political advantage can accrue to the tyrannical.

The point is that there is nothing inherently wrong, or bad, with God's creation. This is a lush and reasonably stable planet upon which to work out the abundant life for all the human beings who inhabit it. For this we should be grateful. The whole problem develops be-cause as yet we haven't learned to live together recog-nizing the right of every human being to life itself and to equal opportunity to enhance that life. This carries us to the second precept that Jesus emphasized.

"Treat others the way you want to be treated," is the most fundamental premise that should underlie all be-havior, all man-made law, all social structures and government itself in any form. This precept is the functional basis of all *natural rights* that have been championed up the centuries. When we have crystal-clear in our minds that we not only live on an impartial planet but that every solitary human being is endowed with the same and equal natural rights, we have true perspective by which to indict the injustices of the present and to provide rational direction to working out all problems. More importantly, such perspective by the individual gives him revitalized incentive in striving for that better and safer society.

So, let us first imbed in our constant thinking that the true rights of human beings are not the laws which man codifies but the unwritten rules, which are inherent in the scheme of life itself. No person comes into life with more rights than any other person nor does he come into life with less rights. Is it difficult to grasp that if each person treated all other persons exactly as he wanted to be treated, "equal justice under the law" would have automatic reality? What person exists who wants to be cheated of his labor, who wants to be physically or mentally injured, or who wants to be denied a role of participation in life that fulfills his needs and constructive urges? Isn't it obvious that the only need for rules is simply that there are those who aren't willing to treat others the way that they themselves want to be treated?

Right here we have the key to all organized society. Men get together and decide on rules that will *prevent* injustice to any of their group. In other words, such organized society has no power to create rights. Such rights have always existed. Every human being is born with them. The constitutions or governments of society are needed instruments only for the purpose of insuring the natural human rights of all participants or members.

IN A MORE tangible and realistic sense the two basic precepts that Jesus emphasized can be directly related to every human being's right to *equal access to Nature's bounty* and every human being's right to *equal opportunity to be a participant in all life.* In both areas it should be noted that it is human beings as living, breathing, aspiring entities that are paramount. Everything else is secondary. Everything else is subordinate.

It is when we now come to trace developing religion and government that we get the full impact of what has happened. Gradually, subtly, almost imperceptibly, the pristine precepts of Jesus have been distorted to the point that life itself has become the slave of all that which is material. In both religion and government, we have come to worship property instead of God, and to enhance material things instead of human beings.

Both the life and teachings of Jesus dealt with compassionate concern for men, women and children, especially the sick and the wayward, those who most needed a helping hand. He himself had no possessions and, further, he admonished the rich that they had as much chance to enter the kingdom of Heaven as a camel passing through a needle's eye. Contrast this with the development of institutionalized religion which has as its main claim to identity, not "fruits by which ye shall know them," but by bigger and more elaborate structures, with softest seats reserved by those able to pay the largest tithes.

Where in the whole of it can one find the precept of "treating others the way you want to be treated"?

When the Founding Fathers set up this nation, they were imbued with the true precepts of Jesus in the ringing words of the Declaration of Independence: "We hold these truths to be self-evident. That all men are created equal; that they are endowed by their Creator with certain unalienable rights; that among these are life, liberty and the pursuit of happiness; that, to secure these rights, governments are instituted among men, deriving their just powers from the consent of the governed; . . . "

The early history of the nation reveals many of the most brilliant forefathers had serious misgivings as to whether the government, set up primarily to insure human rights, might not be inadequate to ward off the dictates of property. They did not live long enough to see that their misgivings were indeed well founded. From a government and a society based on human rights has developed a society dominated by property. Artificial entities of industrial monopolies, financial monopolies and political hierarchies have absolutely taken over the nation. Before the rights of such super-structures, the inherent rights of human beings fade into insignificance. Man has become a slave to things, the victim of his own science.

Human beings, suppressed, abusively restrained in their natural urges or enslaved, will rebel. A society precluding man's sensible inclination to treat others the way he wants to be treated is a society which historically has degenerated to one of ethical break-down and the eruptions of violence. This is what is happening to our nation today. The inherent human rights have been made subservient to the unjust right of property.

Wars violate human rights most flagrantly. Through involuntary servitude, human beings are sent to preserve and defend the "rights of property" through mass killing. No act of man is so in violation of Jesus' precepts as the act of taking the lives of others. Any claim to morality and spirituality in the killing of other human beings is spurious and devoid of rationality. Treating others the way you want to be treated, and loving the Creator with all your might, have in war been denied all validity and all opportunity to function.

Yes, there is a need for the Man of Galilee to speak once again to the hearts of humankind on this planet. And as of old, his question to all men would be the same: "What profiteth it to man if he gain the whole world and lose his own soul?"

~ 11 ~

How About Johnny's Learning to Think?

SUMMER vacation is two-thirds over and come the first week in September over forty million American boys and girls will enroll in the nation's public schools. According to the National Educational Association in its annual report on school statistics which was released in January of this year, it costs the taxpayers over $19,000,000,000 (19 *billion* dollars) to underwrite their education.

During the few remaining weeks before America's teeming offspring make their way into over-crowded classrooms, it might be well for their over-taxed parents to take a candid look at our whole educational system. Perhaps in so doing we may gain a new perspective of the *how, why,* and *what* of education. Certainly, the kind of society we have tomorrow is in direct ratio with the kind of children our educational institutions turn out today!

Before considering education in its intrinsic sense, its true role in any society, let us give a moment's thought to the shallow and warped viewpoint we have of the real purpose of becoming educated or acquiring knowledge. It is a little wonder that our nation gropes and stumbles blindly in shaping its destiny. It has been miseducated to the point where it neither recognizes worthwhile goals nor how to strive for them.

We live in a society that is geared predominantly to the acquisition of material things. Man is not judged by what he knows, what he thinks, or his good intentions toward his fellowmen. On the contrary, he is measured by the size of his home, the horsepower of the car he drives, and the tax-bracket he occupies.

Status symbols have replaced character. True learning has been stifled by conformity.

IT IS this irrational and materialistic society, which came about in the first place through miseducation, that poses the whole problem of inadequate education.

Our children are being trained, not educated, trained to "fit in" and "adjust to" a society that accepts or rejects them on their conformity to standards they lack the ability to evaluate. Our educational institutions, especially those of higher instruction, have simply become mills for the grinding out of "educated" robots to be bargained for in the marts of trade by the highest bidders.

And who are the highest bidders? They are the very monopolistic forces who by abnormal control of the nation's economic, financial and political life not only extract the biggest profits but in whose interest it is to take advantage of adult ignorance and to stereotype young minds.

Tragically, we as a people, the fathers and mothers of the millions of aspiring but unsuspecting boys and girls, have displayed neither the intelligence nor the fortitude to demand major reform of our whole educational system. We have been too hard-pressed in underwriting it with our tax-dollars to give serious thought to the caliber of that which we were underwriting. We, too, have been too busy endeavoring to "fit in" to society to give serious thought as to whether or not the society itself was so constructed as to afford us our just and rightful place.

Right here it should be noted that by no means do we blanketly indict the entire teaching profession. Not only are many serving faithfully without adequate compensation, but also it must be remembered that they must conform to established curricula. To deviate means loss of job. Again, we have economic intimidation.

It is not strange that the whole teaching profession has been undermined. No constructive incentive exists for the nation's teachers to prepare themselves adequately or to apply themselves energetically and conscientiously.

OF RECENT months, Dr. J. D. Koerner, president of the Council for Basic Education, has stressed improper qualifications of teachers. He lays the blame on the teachers' training institutions themselves, which are turning out incompetent graduates. The prospective teacher does not sufficiently understand the subject he has supposedly been trained to teach.

As Dr. Koerner has brought out in his research, the average high school teacher of an academic subject has spent nearly one quarter of his college time taking "education" (how-to-teach) courses. An elementary teacher is even less prepared in subject matter and over-burdened with "education" courses, spending over 40% of undergraduate time with them.

In a recent issue of *The Saturday Evening Post,* Dr. Koerner states that "most of these vices persist because the educational establishment combines the worst features of other protectionist, self-serving bureaucracies while exhibiting few of the virtues of real professional leadership or guardianship of the public interest."

Few parents are aware of the multi-billion-dollar foundations that exert undue pressures on the whole gamut of American education. They are unaware of the fact that there are today more than 15,000 private philanthropic foundations, with total assets of about $13,000,000,000 (*13 billion* dollars) a year in grants, half of it to education.

There are, in fact, 757 foundations with assets of $1,000,000 or more. Is anyone so naïve as to believe that these foundations whose billion-dollar assets were made possible by the ruthless profit-extracting aspect of our economic structure are going to permit education that leads to any constructive reform of that structure? They are about the business of protecting and preserving the goose that lays their golden eggs!

Not all educators are being taken in by the foundation, however. A specific reaction has come from the American Association of School Administrators which includes college presidents, deans, grade and high school superintendents and principals. In a statement issued last February the Association said in part:

"There is a growing uneasiness on the part of many school administrators that perhaps some foundation funds are being used to shape public policy pertaining to education and to promote specific programs at the expense of the curriculum."

A resolution adopted by the Association convention delegates at the same time was even stronger. "Money which they (the foundations) make available is often used as to exert a definite influence on the curriculum."

The Ford Foundation, with assets alone of $2,300,000,-000 and the Rockefeller Foundation with assets of $648,000,000, along with the other large foundations have come under the scrutiny of the Congress. Representative Wright Patman of Texas recently stated that the foundations have reached "massive, undreamed-of proportions" and that it is time for an "agonizing reappraisal" by Congress on how to control them.

What should make each citizen burn with rebellious protest is that not only have these billion-dollar assets resulted from exorbitant profits and price-fixing by giant monopolies but that such assets are tax-exempt. Boiled down to the harsh but inescapable truth, we have an intolerable circumstance. The American taxpayer is picking up the entire tab for the billion-dollar foundations to insure the mis-education of his own children so that they will in turn docilely succumb to the control and dictation of the vested interests.

Even this is not the complete picture. To compound the crime, and it is just that, we as parents are sending our children to school to become mis-educated for jobs that the economic and financial monopolists have made non-existent! Right now when you walk down any average street in America, every sixteenth person you meet is an able-bodied American unable to find work. It is estimated that by the end of the 1960s, 26,000,000 new workers will have entered the labor force during this decade.

Ah, yes, we must be appreciative of our "marvelous educational facilities," of our "free enterprise" system and "unlimited opportunities" for all! We must not be critical, lest we help the Russians! To which we give forth a resounding, Nonsense!"

IT IS high time we get down to real tacks as to just what education should be, what it should embody, and what should be expected of it. When we do, we will understand that we are not dealing with paychecks but with *lives*. We are not dealing with materials but with *human relationships*.

Foremost in our thinking must be the recognition that man is primarily a thinking being and the paramount goal of education is to teach the individual *to think*. A society made up of thinking individuals would equitably resolve every economic and sociological problem through full utilization of all tools and know-how. Maximum profit would accrue to each according to his proportionate contribution to such society. It would be the end of all leeches in society who live off the lifeblood of the majority!

Education is not modern school houses with million-dollar gymnasiums. It is not textbooks as textbooks. Education is simply the imparting and receiving of knowledge, a process of learning. What concerns us is what is imparted, how well it is imparted, and whether each received knowledge increases the ability and comprehension of each individual in maximum, purposeful living!

The great English philosopher of the Victorian Era, Herbert Spencer, stated the heart and core of the whole subject when he wrote, "To prepare as for complete living is the function which education has to discharge." Isn't it apparent that our primary task should not be to "educate" little Johnny so that he can command the *highest salary* in an irrational society, but that as an evaluating, deducing, analyzing entity he can command the *highest respect* in an ultimately rational society?

GENERALLY we are dealing with the millions of children attending public schools but the field of education must include all media, which serve in imparting knowledge to all, irrespective of age group. This includes radio, TV, newspapers, magazines, libraries and informative meetings of all kinds. The same yardsticks that would be applied to youngsters must be equally applied to adults. The most important yardstick is that of approach in accepting knowledge.

The majority are prone to accept information simply on the basis of preponderance of opinion. The majority think a certain way so that is quite all right by me. Secondly, the majority of people are too inclined to accept information, or a stated fact, because it is has been vouched for by authority. They haven't learned to differentiate between so-called "authorities" and so-called "experts".

An authority is simply one who commands attention by virtue of his *position* in society. An expert is one who commands attention by virtue of *knowing* his subject.

It is the third approach, however, that must be underscored. That is the approach of the individual himself in accepting or rejecting all which he partakes of or observes through integrated and balanced thinking. It is the ability to encompass all facts bearing on a problem, attribute relative values to each, and thus be able to arrive at a rational conclusion.

Ninety-nine percent of all the problems we face as a nation today could be solved within a fortnight if the people had the ability to analyze, evaluate and weigh all factors that deal with those problems. We have been propagandized and conditioned into leaving our critical thinking to others. Consequently, the price we're paying is disastrous.

STARTING in the earliest elementary grades the child should be taught that he lives in a Universe of balance and purpose and thus each has the capacity to think and act rationally. He should be taught that this Universe is good and that all know-how and resources, however refined, are for the purpose of serving man to better himself as a cultured and spiritual being. Nowhere is it written on tablets of stone that Man is to be enslaved by his tools or suffocated by increased knowledge.

At an early age the child should have it engrained in his thinking that government, and all social structures, are only for the purpose of implementing the well-being of all individuals. He should have it indelibly etched on his consciousness that the people at all times are dominant and all-powerful. No government possesses proper authority to function that does not conform both to the wishes and consent of the people.

Stretch your imagination to envision 40,000,000 children in our public schools who in varying degrees

recognize their importance as individuals, their unlimited opportunity to pursue an entire lifetime of
satisfying a genuine desire to *know life,* and the right of
each to any station in life he has the capability of
fulfilling. Such an educational atmosphere would leave
little room for worrying about the America of tomorrow.

Unfortunately, such atmosphere and such curriculum
do not spring up by and of themselves. Certainly, the
children cannot and should not assume the responsibility. It lies with the parents of this nation. Along
with economic and political reform, a complete overhaul of our educational institutions is inevitable.

FIRST, sufficient thinking Americans must restore to
the people the direction of their government and economy. Under a Cooperative Commonwealth as provided
in *No More Hunger,* education would be recognized as a
lifetime pursuit. Also it would be recognized that all
education, especially all formal education, would be
available without cost to every individual. God-given
abilities cannot be measured by tuition fees. *There can
be no dropouts in real life!*

Any free and constructive society would encourage to
the *nth* degree man's fulfillment of knowing himself
through knowing all that surrounds him. Education is
that process or opportunity that raises the ability and
comprehension of each in achieving such fulfillment!

Training for jobs that *don't* exist, and kowtowing and
conforming to those that *do exist,* these are the current
goals of education. They are all tied into an economic
and political decay where everyone knows the *price* of
everything but few know the *value* of anything.

115

The first step toward true education, and freedom, is to tear the price tag off each individual and to commence to educate him as a human being.

That is, to be a *thinking* human being!

* * * * *

Thomas H. Huxley **On Education . . .**

THAT MAN, I think, has had a liberal education, who has been so trained in youth that his body is the ready servant of his will, and does with ease and pleasure all the work that, as a mechanism, it is capable of; whose intellect is a clear, cold, logic, engine, with all its parts of equal strength, and in smooth working order; ready like a steam engine, to be turned to any kind of work, and spin the gossamers as well as forge the anchors of the mind; whose mind is stored with a knowledge of the great and fundamental truths of Nature and of the laws of her operations; one who, so stunted ascetic, is full of life and fire, but whose passions are trained to come to heel by a vigorous will, the servant of a tender conscience; who has learned to love all beauty, whether of Nature or of art, to hate all vileness and to respect others as himself. . . .

~ 12 ~

"The Chance To Be Ourselves . . "

By William Dudley Pelley
(Thresholds of Tomorrow)

BUT in the New Day that seems to be coming on America, we're going to arouse to the plights of the thwarted. What is this person striving to become, and how can we help him become it? *We want a whole nation of successful people!*

We want every man and woman in the public domain to be a winner in his or her own right. We don't want misfits, any disgruntled and petulant failures weeping in the sidelines of the nation that they didn't have a chance.

We want all men to have, not only a chance, but a strong assuring public conscience, exercised to see that the least among us has every aid and acclaim to put forth his best and reap the rewards of personal valor. We'll help him to do that, as we want our own selves and our own progeny helped. We'll practice the shibboleth, one for all and all for one, and make it a flaming tocsin.

Friends, what would it mean for this nation if any boy or girl knew in advance that society meant to get behind them, when they became of age, and give them the *maximum advantages* that it was possible to furnish

117

them, to aid them in becoming the thing they desired to be?

WHAT I'm advocating in the provisions of *No More Hunger* is a constitutionally backed system whereby any citizen, man or woman, thrills to the realization that he or she, by reason of having been born or naturalized as an American, has the whole public *soul* behind him or her in attempting to raise himself or herself above the ranks of mediocrity and placing himself or herself on the ascending stairs of achievement, irrespective of age or place of birth or education or marriage or previous handicaps or inhibitions. I don't want more bureaucracy. I want less bureaucracy.

But if you'll study the stipulations of *No More Hunger* you'll learn wherein the individual citizen-soul has his wrists and ankles unshackled to climb as he aspires, with the whole people of his country assisting him, not a government-supported army of stony-faced Do-Gooders to advance or damn him, according as he supports or doesn't support a malodorous national administration in perpetual officeship.

FRIENDS! . . Something extraordinarily beautiful and equitable *must* come out of this nightmare period of propaganda and economic turmoil we've known the past two decades, to balance things up! You and I and all of us, haven't been responsible for this civic diablerie. We've tried to be good citizens and honest workmen, in the main, only asking God and country to give us the chance to prove ourselves and our earnest intent toward our country and our culture. We're willing now, as we've always stood willing in the past, to bear our quota of debt and responsibility for the slings

118

and arrows of international fortune that have afflicted us. But we ask of both life and government *the chance to be ourselves!*

Let's stand up, Gentlemen Unafraid, to this ragtag, bobtailed world of ours and show we can demonstrate the spiritual attainments we've arrived at, with no thanks to anyone but the Divine Father loving all of us!

~ 13 ~

Only the American People Can End the War

By Hugh B. Hester

Peace has no more ardent advocate than Hugh B. Hester, Brigadier General, U. S. Army (retired). Having served in the U. S. Army for over thirty years, he participated in both World Wars and was decorated for gallantry in action by the French and U. S. Governments in WWI. He was also awarded the United States Distinguished Service Medal and the French Legion of Honor for service in WWII. Since his retirement in 1951, he has written and lectured extensively on international relations.

ONE OF THE most encouraging and promising events on the national scene is the recent letter of protest to the President about the Vietnamese War by the student leaders of 100 very important colleges and universities. These leaders and their followers in all the schools throughout the nation, whether in high school, college or graduate school, deserve, it seems to me, the fullest possible support of people everywhere who are for peace and justice.

I do not advise anyone to refuse to serve when conscripted for I cannot serve sentence for him if and when he is convicted for refusing to serve. But I can and do oppose military conscription. And each one of us can and should, I believe, use his influence to the utmost to have it abolished, the war ended, and our boys brought home. The dangerous consequences of military conscription, especially in peacetime, should now be obvious to all. It encourages unwise ventures by those in power. For example, would the United States be involved militarily in Vietnam if peacetime conscription were not in effect? I doubt it.

There has never, in my opinion, been a time when the people of the United States would not have rallied in overwhelming numbers to defend the nation's vital interests and I do not believe there will ever come a time when they would not do so.

For this reason, I oppose all types, of compulsory government service. Many new ones are now being proposed in connection with the review of the present draft laws. The United States needs citizens, not slaves. If the government will make policies worthy of support, it will not need compulsory service of any kind.

The security of the people of the United States is not an issue in the Vietnamese war. The Vietnamese could not attack the United States, even if they wished, because they have no navy or air force capable of doing so, and will not have such force in the foreseeable future. Why then are our young men being conscripted to fight ten thousand miles from home?

Former President Eisenhower, in substance, told the Governor's Conference at Seattle, Washington, August 4, 1953, that we were supporting the French in their war against the Indo-Chinese people because of our need for tin and tungsten and other materials from that area (*New York Times*, August 5, 1953). Senator Gale McGee, Democrat, from Wyoming, confirmed in a Senate speech, February 17, 1965, that it was the vast

121

resources of the area that required our attention (*I. F. Stone's Weekly,* March 1, 1965).

But is this adequate justification for war? Cannot the supplies required by the United States from Southeast Asia, or any other area, be procured at a price fair to the people in those area? I believe they can. Surely, they should not be paid for in the blood of our boys, or by other peoples' sons.

It is vitally important, it seems to me, that this fact be brought to the attention of the American people again and again in order that they may be encouraged to use their sovereignty right to end the war. This can be accomplished through the peoples' representative in Congress. All that is required is Congressional refusal to appropriate the funds for continuing the war.

It is equally important to point out that this does not constitute opposition to our fighting men despite the massive propaganda to that effect. On the contrary, those that oppose the war, in my opinion, are the only friends the fighting forces have. How else can the great slaughter and destruction be stopped except by ending the war?

Sergeant Donald Duncan, the Green Beret, who re-signed after 10 years in the army, 18 months of which were spent in Vietnam, stated, "Those people pro-testing against the war in Vietnam are not against our boys in Vietnam. On the contrary, what they are against is our boys *being* in Vietnam." (*Ramparts,* February 1966).

Sergeant Duncan was so highly regarded as a combat soldier that he was selected at one time to brief Sec-retary McNamara on the war situation in Vietnam. He was also offered a Captaincy, presumably as an inducement to remain in the service. But he declined the promotion and returned to the United States to tell why he opposed the war.

The Washington Administration can secure a cease-fire, according to the National Liberation Front leaders (Viet Cong) and those in North Vietnam, any day it chooses to accept the terms of the Geneva Agreement of 1954. If former President Eisenhower had kept his pledge not to interfere with the implementation of the Geneva Agreement, Vietnam would have been united by free elections and under international supervision in 1956. She would also now be an independent and neutral state. All of these were provided for in the Geneva Agreements, 1954.

If President Johnson would accept the terms of the Geneva Agreements, the war would end almost immediately. And this would in turn help restore the prestige of the United States now so badly damaged by the war. It would also help restore the image of the President as a man of peace, the image upon which he was overwhelmingly elected to office.

The alternatives to the above suggestion are grim indeed. The first and the most dangerous is war with China. For a war with China might very well become World War III, and Journey's End for Man. The second most dangerous alternative, as well as an ignoble one, is the complete destruction of Vietnam and her people. Unfortunately, this is happening now. Unless the American people soon massively protest and stop this war, they will become responsible for the destruction of one of the oldest cultures and societies of man. All that would then be left of this once proud and independent people would be the Quislings, the prostitutes and the miserable refugees.

Should either of these world tragedies occur, the people of the United States would be detested and hated by the vast majority of mankind, as Senator Morse has repeatedly charged, "for the next 500 years."

Postscript

Other High Ranking Officers Oppose the Vietnam War

ACCORDING to an Associated Press release, Febrary 21, 1967, James M. Gavin, Retired 3-star General and former Ambassador to France, told the Senate Foreign Relations Committee we should use the turmoil in China to negotiate peace in Vietnam, but not to escalate the war. Gavin said he believes "we can negotiate with Hanoi and with the National Liberation Front confident that a free, neutral and independent Vietnam can be established with guarantees of stability from an independent body." (Incidentally, all of these were provided for in the Geneva Agreements of 1954.)

Speaking of domestic problems, General Gavin urged that we build a society at home where poverty was abolished and the standard of living was raised for all. He continued, "I emphasize these national needs because I believe that they are being grossly neglected while we continue to escalate our spending in Vietnam."

In the same AP release 4-star General David M. Shoup, former Commandant of the Marine Corps, reaffirmed his opposition to the Vietnam War by stating, "I don't think the whole of Southeast Asia is worth the life or limb of a single American. I believe that if we had and would keep our dirty, bloody, dollar-crooked fingers out of the business of these nations so full of depressed, exploited people, they will arrive at a solution of their own." He continued, "At least what they get will be their own, and not the American style, which they don't want and above all don't want crammed down their throats by Americans."

"The true test of civilization is not the census, nor the size of cities, nor the crops, no, but the kind of man the country turns out."

Ralph Waldo Emerson

~ 14 ~

HAVE WE REACHED THE TURNING POINT?

THE SUMMER just past has afforded Aquila added opportunity to weigh and consider its role in the months ahead. Since the mailing of the July-August issue of *The Eagle's Eye*, there has been extra time to make personal contacts, to attend conventions and do special research. As a consequence, we have gained a more comprehensive picture of the thinking and temperament prevalent throughout America. We want to present here our current evaluations, our outlook and our contemplated efforts.

At the outset we want to state that at no time have we at Aquila been so hopefully optimistic about achieving encompassing social change as we are at the present time. We know that such expression of optimism will seem reckless and irresponsible to many in light of increasing evidences of social and economic breakdown throughout society. However, there is a reasoning and perspective that underlie our hopeful projections for the future.

Ben Franklin once said, "Don't lose heart when things get worse because you are getting closer to the point when they have to turn for the better." There is much truth in this quotation, although it is hardly sufficient in itself to allay the anxieties, the fears, and the genuine concern about a society that seems hell-bent on its own destruction. Confronted with increasing crime, with murder syndicates operating in the nation's commerce, with taxes, indebtedness and foreclosures spiraling unchecked, with ever-increasing bureaucratic dictation, and with this nation's insanity of escalated war in Southeast Asia, few people are able to see hopes for any turning point at all. The majority feel only frustration as to what can be done. To all there seems little ground for any feeling of optimism.

At this juncture, we at Aquila step forward to declare that as a nation *we have reached* the turning point, there is no *lacking* in knowledge as to what should be done, and while it may seem premature to be optimistic, there are nevertheless *substantial and realistic* grounds for envisioning a new order in the affairs of human beings.

Socio-economic system itself causes crime and rebellion

The first thing to take into account is that it is the very fears, the anxieties and the concern of the people that in themselves signify the turning point. For the first time there is an awakening to the stark realization that the nation is in trouble, real and serious trouble. No longer can the mothers and fathers of this nation, as well as its young men and women, dismiss what is happening to their lives as some momentary or temporary disruption. The threats to life itself are too ominous and dangerous. Rebellion, riots and protest bordering on anarchy are erupting throughout the land.

This brings us to the second thing that we have to take into account signifying the turning point. It is this:

Our whole socio-economic system itself has reached the point of no return because it has contained from its beginning the inherent flaws for its own destruction. And right here we need to do some differentiating in order to have a proper perspective.

To date, the larger emphasis, that is, public emphasis, has been on the "problems" of crime, of juvenile delinquency and vandalism, of rioting and anarchistic protest, of "hippies" and drug addicts, of divorce and promiscuity, of apathy and mental breakdown, of both private and public insolvency, and of an involvement in Vietnam where our finest young men are dying in an undefined war.

There has been no public emphasis on the *why*, or the *causes* of the whole spectra of breakdown resulting in a dangerous and sick society.

It is only when we make an honest and objective diagnosis of the real and basic affliction of our nation that we uncover the inescapable disease that has befallen us is the *unworkability of our socio-economic system itself.*

We are forced to face the fact that the violence, crime, rebellion and protest, along with mass poverty, mass indebtedness, and needless wars, are the inevitable denouements of a national framework of working and living which makes the survival and well-being of human beings subordinate to property, profits and despotic power.

They are the result of a framework that turns out more losers than winners. They are the result of a framework, which "legally" but immorally justifies the right of the few to deprive the majority of that which belongs to them. They are the result of a framework which actually provokes crime and evokes rebellion because it has created the irreconcilable circumstance in which serious human needs are unmet while at the same time there exists unused capacity which could meet all those needs abundantly.

It is when the people gain the foregoing perspective that they realize that breakdown has to come before there can be a turning point toward social change that replaces that which is unworkable, unjust and unbearable. No one can preserve a social system from doom and failure that is predicated on economic fallacies and thrives on man's inhumanity to man. Certainly, it is not only unjust but also downright dangerous to condemn and attempt to repress rebellion of people striving to free themselves from tyranny

Half-measures are not sufficient
to restore order and justice

In previous articles we have covered in detail how it is the inequities in our society itself, which spawn crime, and force our teenagers to commit over 50% of the nation's major crimes. We have shown how it is the

very workings of private capitalism, along with private banking control, which deny the people both their rightful purchasing power and rightful ownership in the nation's productive potential, and place both the people and their government in bondage. We have also depicted how our whole political machinery works only in the interest of the oligarchic power structures.

The point to be stressed here is that the increasing crime, the increasing riots, the increasing protest marches, the increasing strikes, the increasing "intellectual" rebellion in all segments of our society, along

129

with the increasing economic instability, and a nation over-extended in a brutal and immoral war, are all evidences that our social-economic-political system is reaching its breaking point.

In reaching the breaking point, we as a nation are also reaching the turning point. At last it is evident to larger and larger numbers that the nation's survival is dependent on looking for broad adjustments in the re-constructing of our whole society. For the first time, there begins to be a willingness to face up to reality. This is the real basis of Aquila's optimism.

Over the years there have been many men and groups who have exposed the fallacies and inequities of our private capitalistic system. Unfortunately they were not heeded, chiefly because the country was so rich and because it was impossible to muster sufficient political strength to bring about change. To generalize, it could be said that the extremely deprived had no means by which to protest and lesser victims had been deceived into believing that somewhere along the line the op-portunity awaited them for their own possession of vast holdings and the power to dominate other human be-ings. It happened just often enough in the days before the fences were built around everything to keep the myth alive.

It must be noted that most expose groups, even today, offer no realistic substitute for the system now in op-eration. They are primarily engaged in pointing out skullduggery and misbehavior in political offices and institutions without recognizing that it is the offices and institutions themselves which permit and encour-age corruption. They fail to see that it is no solution at all merely to replace one set of men with another set of men who in turn are entrapped in an unworkable and corrupting system.

Aquila has reiterated from the time of its inception that there can be no half measures in restoring order out of current chaos and establishing a just and workable economic and social environment. Contacts and inquiries, plus our own research, convince us that the time is here for wide acceptance and endorsement of the Corporate Commonwealth proposal. The temperament and the mood of the nation are such that it wants neither promises nor warmed-over palliatives. The people, especially the young and those excluded from the mainstream of society, want to hear recommendations that deal forthrightly and honestly with their troubles, which are, after all, the problems of the nation.

The Absolute Power of the People

We plead for all who share our convictions to join with us in a concerted program of selling the people of this nation on the goal of an incorporated Commonwealth. And what is our basic presentation to the people? It is simply this:

There is nothing basically wrong with our nation or its people. Nor is there anything wrong with our natural resources and our technological ability. The only thing that is wrong is that we have permitted an economic and political system to crystallize in this nation, which prevents all the people from enjoying the ability of the nation to produce everything to abundance. We have permitted power structures of finance, of industrial monopoly, of military establishments, of political machines to pyramid in our midst until the people have lost all meaningful voice and ownership in their nation.

131

But don't be disheartened or dismayed. Nothing is lost or irretrievable. The subjugators and exploiters of the people have not been able to destroy the inherent and constant right of the people to effect their own liberation. In the hands of the people themselves resides the absolute power to make any and every change to provide for a just and equitable social environment, which will fulfill their needs and allow each individual to develop his own full potential.

We come to you only in the role of counselors. We want you to know that an economic, social and political framework has already been blueprinted, which makes the people absolutely sovereign in working out and shaping their well being. It is premised on the solid foundation of removing all spoils and usurped power from office and unleashing the productive capability of the nation so that each and every human being can enjoy a good home, proper food and clothing, and have full benefit of the nation's capabilities in the fields of medicine and education.

There is no problem in presenting the alternative to the system that is now revealing its unworkableness. It is only a question as to whether you are ready to be arbiters of your own life and that of your children.

Also, there is no problem in making the transition. However, it cannot be achieved by misdirected rebellion in the form of riots, protest marches, or the venting of frustrations in irrational or criminal behavior. Instead of marching **against injustice,** the time has come to march **for justice,** to march for genuine freedom and liberation.

We appeal to every segment of our society, especially those now rebelling, to join in the creation of a citizenry force which ultimately will reach sufficient political strength to constitutionally usher in a New Order in the affairs of the sovereign people.

The keynote of the whole effort will not only be enlightenment as to the fallacious premises and injustices of private predatory capitalism but more importantly as to the sound and just premises of a cooperative, corporate Commonwealth. It is imperative that such enlightenment underlie all our efforts. From such enlightenment will come the irrepressible inspiration and drive to achieve our goals while at the same time it will insure and sustain our goals when they have become reality.

This is broadly our message to the people of this nation. In the weeks and months ahead we at Aquila will be initiating specific actions. This will necessitate setting up study groups, making personal contacts and broadening our whole scope of activity.

We at Aquila are unshakably convinced that a Corporate Commonwealth is "an idea whose time has come!"

How about you?

~ 15 ~

Why Money Is Going Out Of Business

THERE WAS a time in this nation when the average person looked askance at any substitute for good, old "cold cash." Sheer possession of literal currency in one's sweaty little fist somehow made ownership of purchasing power that much more secure and realistic. "Put that green stuff on the barrelhead if you want to make a deal" was the self-assuring approach to any transaction.

The five, the ten, the twenty-dollar bill in one's actual possession gave one the physical "feel" of money. Of course, the soundness or validity of such cold cash, whether or not it reflected true wealth, never crossed the possessor's mind. How it came into circulation, and how its supply was determined, were totally outside his interest or speculation.

With the passage of the Federal Reserve Act in 1913 the bank demand-deposit, or "check," became the major paper instrument by which the nation's business was conducted. The facility with which it could be employed mushroomed its use into covering over 90% of all dealings and purchases. As with cash circulation, the average person posed no serious questions as to the soundness and validity of the "credit" dollars, which he was using. He was content in the knowledge that

134

everyone else was employing checks and they were acceptable in exchange for both goods and services.

Not having any understanding of how his money was created, or more importantly, how the amount of money was arbitrarily determined, the average citizen has over the years been satisfied to accept the promoted fiction that both his cash and checks were backed by gold. While it is true that prior to 1934 the legal right existed to convert both currency and bank deposits into gold, no such amount of gold has actually existed.

For example, when the Federal Reserve was organized in 1914, the total deposits and currency in circulation amounted to 20 billion dollars, but there was only 1.6 billion dollars of monetary gold in the country. In other words the amount of money in circulation was 12 times the amount of gold. According to figures from the House Committee on Banking and Currency, a similar proportion held true some fifty years later in 1963. At t;hat time the money supply, both cash and checks, totaled 157.4 billion dollars and the Treasury's gold was only 15.6 billion dollars.

However, citing these figures is begging the point. In 1934, the private banking institutions succeeded in pushing through a law that not only made it illegal to possess gold but no American citizen could demand gold in exchange for his dollars. As usual, of course, there was an exemption for the non-American. Foriegners holding American credit could through their banks demand and have their dollars converted into gold.

This is the same double-standard as obtains when a foreign government, often headed by an outright dictator, gets a U. S. government loan with a ten-year moratorium on the principle that carries only 1-1/2% interest, while a native American must pay 6% interest and make immediate payments on the principal. If the foreign borrower refuses to repay his loan, it is simply entered as a "bad debt" while the small farmer, the small businessman or the homeowner must relinquish his property.

Throughout the monetary history of this nation the private banks have promoted the calculated deception that gold is the only sound basis of a nation's money supply. The fact that such basis permitted them to control the money supply simply by cornering the gold supply was carefully kept from the people. What should have registered with the people with shocking impact is this challenging question: If the whole purpose of a money supply is to facilitate the exchange of goods and services, and to provide for productive expansion, why then shouldn't all money be related directly to those goods, services and production?

What twisted reasoning dictates that a nation's progress and well-being should be dependent on some mystic quality of a metal instead of being directly dependent on the resources, manpower and ingenuity of the whole nation and its people?

From a private banking system based on worthless bags of gold, we have come supinely to accept an entire money supply based on debt. Not one person in a thousand, nay, not one in a hundred thousand, recognizes the gargantuan hoax that the private bankers have perpetuated on the nation, its citizens and its government. Unsuspectingly, the people and their government have turned over their property and their

136

earning capacity to the private banks to be lent back to them in the form of interest-bearing debt.

Slowly but surely, more and more people are coming to recognize the fallacious gimmick of "fractional-reserve" lending which permits the private banks to grant loans, bear in mind that it is the people's credit that makes the loans good, equal to five times the assets or reserves of the bank itself. All such granting of loans, or credit-dollars, is nothing but the *manufacture of money.* Every time a loan is made, this is money that had no existence prior to its creation by the private bank.

This arbitrary power to expand and contract the money supply by the making of loans or calling them in has placed in the hands of the private bankers the unhallowed power not only to change the value of the purchasing worth of the dollar but has given them the power literally to determine the amount of work the nation can do. *The nation's entire working capacity has been made beholden to the whim and greed of those who are non-producers!*

It has been under such controlled economy that the people and their government have had to go deeper and deeper into strangling debt. Thus came into practice the whole gamut of installment buying with exorbitant carrying charges. Then came credit cards of a thousand varieties. In buying merchandise or in having the family car filled with gas, one simply presented one's credit card. At the end of the month a bill arrived from the respective company and one sent in a remittance covering partially or fully the month's purchases.

While in the past much of installment buying was turned over to the banks for credit handling, the private banks had stayed out of the actual credit card business. Into the picture they have now come with full gusto. Of recent time, millions of citizens in the Midwest have been receiving unsolicited letters from their local banks enclosing "personal charge cards" and informing them that these cards can be used in making purchases in more than 60,000 merchants' establishments. The recipient is told that his "Town and Country Charge Card" has been subscribed to by over 450 banks and he can present it to any merchant displaying the Midwest Bank Card symbol, a stylized dollar in a circle.

Town and Country Charge is one of a dozen individual charge card plans in the Midwest System. The system is designed ultimately to enable a cardholder of any Midwest Bank Card plan to use his charge card at participating merchants' stores throughout the Midwest. Sales slips are exchanged among banks, much as checks are exchanged. Each month the holder of a Charge Card receives a statement from his bank which he may pay in full or pay in monthly installments on a revolving credit system for which he is assessed a carrying charge.

The whole projection of banking into the credit card business has stimulated much mixed reaction. One writer in the Midwest stated, "Cheers, jeers, fears, greet bank credit card." There is considerable speculation as to the increase in irresponsible spending by insatiable consumers, the need for government to intercede by setting up Federal agencies to regulate credit activities, and the ultimate setting up of central credit bureaus which would be an invasion of everybody's privacy.

We at Aquila are observing this whole promotion of the bank credit card with two specific reactions:

First, we recognize that the entire present approach is nothing but another step by a seriously faltering economy to preserve itself by increased indebtedness. Not one iota of genuine purchasing power, based on added production, is being interjected into the economy. A people already in private debt of over $900,000,000,000 (*nine hundred billion dollars*) are being seduced into spending what they do no possess. At the same time the private banks not only collect their compounding carrying charges but expand their control over the lives of every citizen.

A local merchant told Aquila that if he became a member of the bank charge card system, he would have to pay $5 out of every $100 of sales in order to participate. While the local bank magnanimously points out that there will be no cost to the person using a bank charge card, provided of course that he pays each monthly statement in full, it neglects to point out that every time a person makes a purchase he is actually paying a hidden cost in the form of increased prices necessitated by the merchant's increased overhead.

However, it is Aquila's second reaction to be most intrigued and full of far-reaching speculation. From a money system of circulating cash and credit, all based on debt, the nation has taken a giant step toward an "accounting system" of banking. Already we hear such system identified as a "cashless and checkless" society. Of course, at present, it is wrongly engineered, wrongly controlled, and wrongly premised. Yet in principle it presages the only sound system of exercising purchasing power in a technological, abundant society.

We have stressed over and over again that a nation's banks should be nothing but clearing houses for keeping a running account of each person's earned claim against all the goods and services produced by the nation. Simultaneously, we have also stressed that such claims should be based on not only the people's human effort but on their rightful, inherent equity in the nation's entire resources and productive capacity. From the nation's very inception, but particularly with the American industrial revolution starting in the 1850's, the economic structure of private capitalism has systematically concentrated the wealth and producing assets of the nation in the hands of bigger and bigger power structures.

It is when one understands to what degree all the people have been denied their rightful equity in the resources, the accumulated technology, and the actual producing machinery of the nation that one grasps to what degree the people and their government have had to go into irretrievable bondage to the private debt-merchants. It has been a satanic process of a nation's mortgaging its future earning power, in the form of loans, liens, credit and the whole spectrum of vampiristic interest, in order that it might buy that which it in the accumulate has already produced.

Could anything be more idiotic and self-defeating, and more self-destroying?

There can be no solution to the nation's economic problems until every human being in this nation has equity in the nation's total ability to produce. From an economy of *private* capitalism must be ushered in an economy of *public* capitalism. We contend that if private capitalism, stock ownership of the producing assets of the nation, is sound and proper for providing the abundant life for a small segment of our society, then an expansion of that framework to encompass every citizen as a dividend-receiving stockholder in this nation is equally sound and proper. This, of course, is the basic premise of the Corporate Commonwealth.

With the total citizenry having equity in the nation's total ability to produce everything to abundance, it should be obvious that it would at all times have earned claims, or purchasing power, against all goods and services in direct balance. More goods and more services would automatically mean a direct proportionate increase in purchasing power. Such purchasing power would be the nation's money supply. The pertinent question then simply become: What form shall it take?

The answer lies in the complete elimination of private banking and its fallacious circulating cash and credit and the substitution of nation-wide Commonwealth Accounting System in which each citizen commands a credit-account equal to his share in the nation's business. The citizen presents his inviolate credit card as he makes each purchase and a notation of the sale is forwarded to the Commonwealth Accounting Bank to be deducted from the citizen's over-all credit. It is as simple as that.

The workability of this innovation has, of course, been made possible by modern technology and electronic communication. The ironical thing is that it has been the exploding development of knowledge in the way of producing and communicating which has exposed the flagrant and abusive flaws in the whole economy. Private banking and producing monopolies were able to camouflage their despotic control under an economy, which has the potential to produce abundant life for all citizens; their control has become unmanageable.

Re-read the chapter in *No More Hunger,* which is entitled, "Where the Dividends Come From" and you will get a clearer perspective of the only true role that money should play in a just and equitable economy. The fact is this nation doesn't need any of the debt-money of the usurers, and they have real cause for the jitters!

The adamant foundation of a Corporate Commonwealth is that there cannot be true political sovereignty without first economic sovereignty!

"As a result of the war, corporations have been enthroned and an era of corruption in high places will follow and the MONEY POWER of the country will endeavor to prolong its reign by working on the prejudices of the people until wealth is aggregated in the hands of the few and the Republic is destroyed. I feel at this moment more anxiety for the safety of my country than ever before, even in the midst of war."

—— Abraham Lincoln

~16 ~

The Unholy Trinity!

FOR almost three years we have published *The Eagle's Eye.* During that time we have perhaps devoted too much space to the problems that beset the nation without allowing sufficient space to the basic social reform we are advocating. As a consequence, we continue to find readers who have only a vague and shadowy picture of what we are endeavoring to actualize in America.

In one article it is impossible to fully support the contentions that will be made. However, the main purpose of this presentation is simply to highlight our primary objectives. We want you to get the broad picture of what must be done before law and order, equity and integrity can be restored to this land.

Anything short of what we seek will solve no major problems and is but self-deception.

Three major areas concern us. As goals they would be stated as follows:

1. A sovereign people must assume their inherent decision-making prerogative and pass directly on all legislation and policy affecting their lives and their future.

2. A sovereign people must assume the issuance of their own money.

3. A sovereign people must assume their rightful, earned equity in the resources and productive assets of the nation.

THESE ARE the major goals of Aquila. These are the major pieces of surgery that must be done on the nation if the nation's health is to be restored. Achievement of both such surgery and goals is the dynamic role of a NATIONAL COOPERATIVE COMMONWEALTH. Its adoption will bring about a meaningful opportunity for all people to live harmoniously and prosperously together.

Political parties, private banking and minority ownership of a nation's productive capacity are the cancerous growths that are responsible for the malnutrition of many millions, for the incapacitation of other millions, and for the mental breakdown that involves yet other millions in violence. They are the deadly diseases that are sapping the last ounce of vitality from the 190,000-000 cells that make up the national body.

Paupers, dope addicts, criminals, the jobless, the ignorant, and the insane are the living testimonials to the nation's sick condition. Add to this a nation that is going in debt at a rate *five times* faster than its rate of producing goods and services, plus the fact that there now exists in the world nuclear explosives equvivalent to 500 tons of TNT for every man, woman and child on this planet, and one need not say anything more to prove the corruption, immorality and insanity of our system and its methods.

THERE is a need for remedies that scour. It is too late for palliatives or diagnosis that deal only with the symptoms and ignore the diseases. Either the people face up to the real causes of their nation's illness or they must accept needless deterioration of both body and mind leading inevitably to self-destruction.

In the individual case, any doctor will state that half the battle in overcoming an affliction is the *will to live*. This is doubly true in respect to a nation. If we at Aquila didn't believe the people do have the will to live, *to fight* for their survival and well being, there could be no purpose in our efforts.

The first step of a people determined to survive is to recognize that out of political parties do not come the spokesman of the people. From the lowest ward heeler at the bottom to the political chieftain at the top, political candidates are chosen by vested interests to do their bidding. This is not to say that there aren't exceptions to the circumstance but such mavericks are powerless to speak effectively for the people who elected them.

To any suggestion that political parties, or our so-called "two-party system," are sacrosanct, we give forth with a thunderous refutation. They are the front-men for the power-blocs entrenched in our midst and have been interjected between the people and their government purposely to thwart the will of the electorate. To look for alleviation of a nation's ills through politicians is the same as going to the exploiters themselves and pleading that they relinquish their unearned profits and usurped power. The folly and futility of such pleading should be apparent.

Where then does the power for action come from? It comes from the citizens themselves who inherently possess it *constantly*. The fact that the people may have unthinkingly or unwisely delegated power to a few does not alter one iota the fact that the absolute power rests in the hands of the people to withdraw such delegation and henceforth to be the direct arbiters of their destiny. There is none to stay their hands.

In previous articles we have covered in more detail the need for the people to pass directly on all major legislation. Elected representatives should be chosen from a *publicly* underwritten campaign, candidates contending with each other on TV forums, and those elected should be restricted to the role of *recommending* legislation.

It is time to recognize the overwhelming historical proof that "power tends to corrupt, and absolute power corrupts absolutely."

For the moment the important point to imbed in your consciousness, and to entertain every moment of your waking hours, is that neither men nor institutions, nor laws, not even the Constitution itself, are beyond modification by the people. The timidity, and ignorance, that precludes a sovereign people from making those changes that would affect a better and more equitable society, are the earmarks of slaves not freemen!

The inherent power of a people should always be exercised intelligently. It cannot be so exercised unless they have the understanding of the two other major areas of usurped power that we mentioned: Monetary control and productive monopoly. These coupled with political-military power are the unholy trinity for the enslavement of mankind.

IT IS HOPED that every reader either sent for the material covering the investigation of the Federal Reserve System from Representative Wright Patman, chairman of both the House Committee on Banking and Currency and the Subcommittee on Domestic Finance, or requested the material from his own Congressman. If you did, and if you read the material, there is little that need be said here about the unconstitutional and vampiristic control of the nation's money supply by private banking institutions.

In the past, students of the money question had to rely on their own observations, with a minimum of direct testimony of the bankers, to expose the power and machinations of those who *manufacture* money. The importance of the recent congressional investigation is that the same evidence, and much more, is now supported by the testimony of the bankers themselves. For the first time in the history of the nation the top moguls of the entire banking fraternity were made to testify under oath regarding their clandestine functioning.

It marked a milestone in the struggle for monetary reform.

There are many ramifications to private banking and its throttling of the entire economy, its extracting of hundreds of billions of dollars in unearned profits through interest and foreclosures, but the injustice and wrongness of the whole predatory system can be stated simply. It is this:

The people have turned over their credit, represented in possessions and earning power, and their nation's credit, represented by the nation's total worth, to the private banks to be rented back to the people in the form of debt upon which they have to pay a tribute called interest.

147

From this circumstance several pertinent facts should be obvious. First, one should be struck by the realization that every dollar that is put into circulation is in the form of interest-bearing indebtedness. The individual must give the bank his mortgage. The government must give the banks its bonds. The banks give no equivalent value in return and take no risk.

As aforementioned, they are in the exploitive and lucrative business of loaning to the people the people's own credit.

Secondly, a more disturbing fact reveals itself. The privately owned banks have the exclusive power to determine the amount of money in circulation. By expanding and contracting the money supply they not only control the amount of jobs, the extent of business, and the degree of work the nation can perform, but they arbitrarily determine the purchasing value of every dollar earned and every dollar spent.

There is no power on earth as formidable and evil as the private control of a nation's money. Such control leads not only to wholesale indebtedness but inevitably leads to oligarchic control of both a nation's industry and government itself. It is sheer stupidity to speak of social reform and give no thought to the ruthless power of private banking.

Note the contrast in the functioning of money under a Cooperative Commonwealth. It contends: if the individual's and the nation's credit is sufficient upon which the private banks can put money in circulation why then cannot a sovereign people provide for all their monetary needs based on the same credit without incurring a dollar of debt or paying one cent in interest? Of course it can be done and the usurers have the jitters that the people might awaken and usher in such innovation.

Under such sound money the nation could utilize all its resources and its most advanced technology to produce and abundance of both goods and services for the good life for every citizen. At last the economy would be unshackled. Money, or purchasing power, would automatically come into circulation as work *was* done. No longer would a sovereign people have to crawl to non-producing financiers and beg to have them relinquish the people's own credit.

Take a good look at the next multi-million-dollar bank in your vicinity and see if one productive machine is located on the premises. Private bankers are debt-merchants and must be recognized as such.

Under a new dispensation in the affairs of men, banking will be solely a service of clearing and tabulating the *earned* accounts of the nation's citizens. It will be a public institution owned and operated by the government of the people.

BRIEFLY, let us consider the third area dealing with monopolistic cartels. Statistics and evidence exists to surfeit that the productive assets of the nation have become lodged in the hands of a small group of giant corporations. Such evidence bears out that less than *three percent* of the corporations in the nation account for *ninety percent* of all production and services.

The latest *Fortune Directory* lists the 500 largest corporations of the 300,000 in the nation. These top 500 manufacturing corporations have assets totaling 224.6 billion dollars, exceeding *three times* the assets of all the other corporations *combined*. Increased profits and expansion indicate accelerated concentration of the nation's whole productive capacity.

The same picture, and trend, is similarly evident in *Fortune's* listing of the fifty largest commercial banks, the fifty largest life insurance companies, the fifty largest merchandising firms, the fifty largest transportation companies, and the fifty largest utilities. All showed marked increase in both exorbitant profits and assets. Like the industrial companies, these corporations dominate the market in their respective fields.

In the meantime, the small manufacturer, the small retailer, the small farmer are increasingly being eliminated. Denied the advantage of the latest technology, and denied full access to the market place because of their enforced smallness, "fair competition" is but a farce and a delusion to the small operator struggling to compete.

For the people and their government, the nation's ultimate ability to produce everything to abundance has meant only increased indebtedness and insolvency. Thus the tragic and unjust disparity existing throughout the nation. On the one hand there are booming times for the few. On the other, bankruptcy or exclusion from useful function for the many.

Such inequitable disparity has not happened overnight. Nor has it resulted from natural causes. It has been the progressive, inevitable denouement of private capitalism from the beginning. Under the camouflage of "free enterprise" we as a nation have permitted individuals and corporations to extract earnings and to accumulate assets on a premise other than some form of human effort. This fallacious premise has been identified as the "profit" system.

In operation this system has simply been the license for the shrewd and ruthless to extort *unearned* income from the labor and industry of the majority. With this economic advantage came the garnering of the nation's assets and control of its whole economy.

There was only one course for the disadvantaged citizenry to follow in order to survive. This was to go hopelessly in debt. To the exact degree that they had had their earnings stolen from them they must mortgage their future to buy what they had produced in the present. The magnitude of such "legalized" extortion now exceeds over $2,000,000,000,000 *(two trillion dollars!).* And it is rising. . . .

AQUILA states unequivocally that the people can never enjoy the fruits of a free society until all the people have their rightful equity in, and claims against, the nation's maximum ability to produce all goods and services. Make no mistake, it has been the tens of millions of workers, the tens of millions of consumers, and the tens of millions of taxpayers who have in the main paid for the building of the nation's entire productive capacity. They cannot be excluded from that which they and their forebears all helped to make possible.

The basic feature of a Cooperative Commonwealth is to restore the people's equity in the assets of the nation. Its goal is to make every citizen a voting "capitalist" in the democratic functioning of his nation, both economically and politically. Every individual, irrespective of his color or origin, has an earned and inherent right to be a meaningful participant.

151

There need be no upheaval in the use of our technology and coordinated bigness. In fact, unused science and resources should be immediately put to work in insuring the abundant and good life for all citizens. Most import of all, in the hands of the people would reside the decision-making power to protect the future interests of not only themselves but also that of their children.

Only achievement of the foregoing major innovations will install a leadership that strives for peace in the world above everything else. Currently American boys are dying to export to foreign soil the same ills that the "military-industrial" complex has succeeded in foisting on America.

We have only sketchily given you a picture of what we seek through our efforts. Past articles cover, and future articles will cover, more details. In this article we wanted to cover the specific challenges that confront the nation.

Aquila wants nothing to do with either capitalism or communism. It is a New Order in the affairs of free men that must be ushered in. It is new concepts of working together, playing together, and learning together that must be embraced.

To those who say, "We are in accord with all you say, and stand for, but the people are helpless to bring about such advocated social change," we simply retort: "In the hands of the people rests the supreme power to effect all social change that will insure their survival and happiness."

There need be no histrionics or mincing of words. Those who will not join with others in fighting for their own liberation, and that of their children, deserve to be slaves to the "unholy trinity" that have them in bondage!

The decision is in the hands of the people!

As I would not be a slave, so I would not be a master. This expresses my idea of democracy."

---Abraham Lincoln

~ 17 ~

"If any man serve me, let him follow me!"

ANOTHER CHRISTMAS is upon us. Outwardly, it is but a repetition of all that the nation has experienced in the past. Only there is more of everything. Everywhere one looks there are added trappings and trimmings. More wreaths are hung from doorways, more multi-color lights illuminate city squares, and more gift-wrapped parcels are in evidence. More carols fill the air and more chimes toll incessantly in the distance.

We are smothered by the superficiality of the whole of it.

In all solemnity, and candor, we ask, "Where is the Prince of Peace really represented? Where is there meaningful commemoration of the Man whose birthday is being recognized? Where is there manifestation of the dynamic precepts He enunciated during his ministry?"

Lest we be accused of being Old Scrooges, we are not unmindful of the general merriment of the occasion. We know that for many it is a time of momentary respite from the cares and ugliness of the world around us. Even for the poorest children it is one of eager anticipation for Santa's arrival, and for adults it is a time of giving to others. We, too, are moved by the clear and resonant rendition of "Silent Night" by the children's choir and sincere people acclaiming "Peace on Earth, good will toward men." Yet, all is but momentary symbolism of the Man whose life was dedicated to Peace, and whose every act demonstrated His concern and compassion for the lowliest among men.

ACROSS the breadth and length of this nation over 300,000 churches dot the landscape and are located on thoroughfares. Each Sunday, and often during the week, tens of millions attend these churches. Week in and week out they listen to men who mount pulpits purportedly to show mankind how to walk in the footsteps of the Man who stands at the pinnacle of their religion. What a hollow mockery such institutionalized religion has made of the teaching of this Man who walked the shores of Galilee!

It is not our intention to pass any final judgment on organized Christianity because even at the moment it is in the throes of evaluating its own dereliction. Nor do we intend too harsh an indictment of its membership who fill church coffers with over three billion dollars annually. It, too, is showing apprehension over the dearth of spirituality demonstrated. At the same time we want none of the hypocrisy that pleads allegiance to the Prince of Peace and does nothing tangible or realistic in applying His precepts for mankind's betterment.

As for Christmas it is our belief that the Prince of Peace would have no toleration for any of the seductive commercialism, and would have only a bemused toleration for the perennial myth of a fat man sliding down a chimney. It is our belief that He would be little impressed even with the pageantry depicting his birth in a Bethlehem stable. For He, more than anyone else, knew that the dynamism of His mission had little to do with how He was born, or how He endured, or for that matter how He died.

It had everything to do with *how He taught people to live.* . . .

MANKIND has strayed far afield from the teachings that He voiced nearly two thousand years ago. His followers have enshrouded His words with piety and have beclouded the meaningful import of His precepts as to how man should treat man in all relationships. From a philosophy of mutual love, mutual respect, and mutual understanding, wherein true self-attainment could be realized through service to others, there has come to pass a philosophy of every one for himself with moral justification for the acts of the cunning, the brutal and the arrogant.

If the Prince of Peace appeared in our midst today, two broad areas would command His direct and uncompromising attention. The first is a world torn by war, permeated with violence and displaying callous indifference to the preciousness of life itself. The second would be all circumstances within which the few can disservice the majority with resultant oppression stultifying the spiritual growth of the individual.

It was on these two major areas that He focused all his teachings. It is in these two areas that Twentieth Century man has flouted all that He epitomized and practiced.

The whole essence of Jesus' preachment was the potential goodness, and intrinsic worth, of each and every human being. He recognized the capacity for love

156

in all men and to those who faltered or "sinned," He offered forgiveness and inspired them to mend their ways. He saw in ignorance, misery and violence the only real enemies of man. "Love thy God with all thy might, and treat others the way that you wish to be treated" was the crux and shibboleth of His whole message.

IN A WORLD of hate, of lust, of violence, with hundreds of millions of fellow human beings condemned to death because of needless poverty and disease, and with a whole world geared to its own annihilation, it is sheer hypocrisy to plead adherence to the teachings of the Prince of Peace. Blind loyalty and unpracticed belief are no substitutes for his criterion "By their fruits ye shall know them," or, "If any man serve me, let him follow me!"

It could be that it is the profound simplicity of the doctrine voiced by the Man of Nazareth that is the main barrier to its acceptance. It is much easier, and more expedient, to judge men outwardly rather than inwardly. Instead of recognizing the immortality and intrinsic worth of every human as a product of a Beneficent and Impartial Creator, we condemn him because of his skin color, his momentary government, or the particular social arrangement that dictates his behavior. Lost is the individual's inherent right to life and his God-given prerogative to exist irrespective of mortal differences.

The whole premise of Jesus' ministry was the attainment of the Brotherhood of Man by rationality and manifest altruism. His every act and admonition deplored self-righteousness and decried the use of vio-

157

lence to make men good and compassionate. Perhaps He summed it up best when He said, "Whosoever therefore shall humble himself as this little child, the same is greatest in the kingdom of heaven. And whoso shall receive one such little child in my name receiveth me. But whoso shall offend one of these little ones which believe in me, it were better for him that a millstone were hanged about his neck, and that he was drowned in the depth of the sea."

TODAY, we the people of America have more than a responsibility to ourselves and the world. As the most powerful nation in the world, we have transcendent opportunity to stand in the vanguard for the realization of "peace and good will among all men." First, however, we must make honest appraisal of the disorder, the injustice and the violence in our own household. In so doing, we would find it irreconcilable to have American boys bleeding and dying to give freedoms to others, which have no actuality in America.

Only as we can see that reason and compassion can restore tranquility and justice and order to our own nation, can we truly comprehend how they can restore peace and equity to other nations. There is only one weapon for the combating of inequity and violence and that is understanding tempered with love for one's fellowmen. It is the only workable force for the negotiating of all differences and the achievement of the good and safe life for all mankind. Not only is it the common denominator of all life but it is double-edged in reaching the heart of both giver and recipient.

The world stands at the crossroads. In man's hands are the tools and science to create a literal burning Hell or a Paradise on earth. There is no alternative to a cessation of all hostilities, complete disarmament and peace. A people who cannot live together must die together.

How fleeting and hypocritical to set aside one day each year to commemorate the life of the Prince of Peace! If man would survive, he must belatedly recognize the significance of what He taught, not only each month, but throughout the whole year. But more than this. His precepts must be applied so universally that every newborn child, in every part of the world, can have the love and nurturing of all mankind in living its life to fullest unfoldment.

In that day we can truly pray, "Thy will be done in earth, as it is in Heaven."

CHRISTMAS, 1965

May the message of Him whose birthday we mark sound as a clear trumpet call above earth's clamor, confusion and change.

Let there be peace where there has been war.

Let there be courage where there has been fear.

Let there be faith where there has been dispair.

May Jesus' love for all mankind awaken a million answering echoes in our hearts.

And may the New Year mark the upward turning of mankind's path toward a New and Better Age.

~ 18 ~

The Fourth Branch of Government . . . The People!

STARTING with the October issue of the magazine we commenced a series of three articles. It was our intention to present progressively the broad, fundamental premises upon which to base all our economic, political and social thinking. At the outset we realized that much by sheer limitations of space would remain unsaid and should be stated. Also, we were aware that too brief an enunciation of fundamentals often shape up as mere platitudes in the mind of the reader and have no realistic value.

Nevertheless, wse decided to undertake the writing of the series with the strong conviction on our part that ninety-five percent of the misconceptions and erroneous thinking about human relationships, in all aspects of life, stem from faulty premises. How can the individual determine his right to employment, his right to education, his right to all the good things which we have the capacity to produce to abundance, and his right to live wholesomely and with dignity, if he doesn't understand his inherent claims against organized society? How can he be judge for himself on the inequities of prevailing economic and political structure if he doesn't grasp the rights that are his? Lastly, how can he be persuaded to embrace social improvements if he doesn't comprehend the indisputable premises upon which man's betterment can be shaped and promoted?

In the October issue we endeavored to erase from anybody's thinking that we are hapless victims of a cruel and unjust Universe in which death is the only surcease to paying off the mortgage, struggling to keep employed, buying Junior's shoes, and sending Mary to college. We wanted to make it plain that we are the inhabitants of a Good and Rational Universe that is bountiful both in raw ingredients and unlimited levels of energy out of which can be fashioned to surfeit the necessities and comforts of every human being. We wanted particularly to impress you with the inescapable fact that there was no divine stipulation allocating resources, parceling up the planet, or giving any one or any group, the right to build fences around the bounty of Natue and preclude the majority from enjoying the good and secure life that is possible.

In the same vein, we emphasized that all accumulated knowledge up the centuries is likewise a legacy of all the people. Not only the scientists and other learned men throughout history that have contributed to the pyramiding of knowledge and perfecting of tools, but billions of people have preceded the present living who made their contributions in less spectacular but just as necessary roles. Should the benefit from all such contributions redound to only a favored few in society, or does all such knowledge and hard work belong to all the people?

LEADING off in the November issue we tried to drive home the fact that no individual is born with more, or less, rights than any other individual. On this basis each person should recognize his claim, as a human being, against all material wealth in the sense of his irrevocable right to expend effort, or having the inherited benefit of our technology, in owning his own home, providing for all his medical needs, enjoying a standard of living commensurate with the nation's ability to produce.

We went further. We emphasized that every human being has an equally irrevocable right to be a participant in society, constantly developing his character, knowledge and innate abilities to the utmost. We pointed out that this right embodied the undeniable right to equal educational opportunities irrespective of financial capability, skin color, or station in life. How else could each child become equipped to play his role in society on the same footing as any other person? We particularly stressed that each person has an inherent right to participate politically. No person can be compelled to abide by rules, laws or institutions whose regulatory power he never sanctioned.

To this point we have purposely refreshed your mind on the basic thinking of the two previous articles so that you could get the full impact of the premise presented in this article. A Good and Rational Universe is of little importance to the average citizen if predatory and monopolistic power-blocks have corralled the majority of the natural resources into their hands. The productive potential, made possible through the contributions of all people, is of little importance if tens of millions are impoverished, million can't obtain employment, and the people have no equity or control of the vast machinery that can produce more cars, more refrigerators, more food, more clothing, and more luxuries than all

162

the people can humanly enjoy, excluding not a solitary citizen.

In short, what practical value is there in accentuating the importance of each and every human being and enunciating his inherent rights if they can't be translated into meaningful exercise? Here is when the third, and perhaps the most dynamic premise, underlying all human relationships must be considered and grasped. It is simply this:

In the people's hands rests the supreme power

It is the people who have the inviolate power to effect any change or renovation in economic and political structure that they deem necessary to protect and enhance their inherent rights as human beings. People don't have to suffer injustice, inequity or unnecessary hardships one moment longer than they are willing to modify or eliminate those strictures that prevent them from enjoying a just and full life. It must become crystal clear in everyone's thinking that institutions, laws and government itself have authority only as they equitably and honestly serve in implementing the well being of all the people and unreservedly protect the rights of every human being!

THERE is no clearer enunciation of this fundamental premise than what is set down in the Declaration of Independence: "That to secure these rights, governments are instituted among men, deriving their just powers from the consent of the governed. That whenever any form of government becomes destructive of these ends it is the right of the people to alter or to abolish it, and to institute new government, laying its foundation on such principles and organizing its powers in such form, as to them shall seem most likely to effect their safety and happiness." Thus spake the Founding Fathers who subsequently adopted a Constitution which starts off with these significant word, *"We the people* of the United States, in order to form a more perfect Union . . . "

The foregoing is not cited, nor should be interpreted, as any advocacy of abolishing our Constitution. More to the point, it is cited to impress on our minds that these two major documents laying the foundation for governmental and economic structure set forth unmistakably the supreme power of the people not only in the literal functioning of society but in altering unjust or inadequate provisions. It is tragic that such limited conception of the people's role is entertained by most citizens who bemoan their helplessness to effect social change.

Attend any political rally, sit in the classroom of any course on government, or read any conventional exposition dealing with our government, and one is left with the conclusion that there are only three distinct branches provided by the Constitution. Most Americans are satisfied to accept that the Constitution simply provides for a **legislative** branch, which makes the laws, an **executive** branch, which carries out the laws, and a **judicial** branch, which interprets the laws. To this self-contained government package is attached the schematic label that the three branches serve as a check and balance on each other, and outside of the citizens wending their way to a voting booth every two and four years the whole mechanism of government is self-operating.

It is startling to the average student and to the average adult citizen to be told that the most important branch of government has not even been mentioned. In fact, the mere suggestion of such exclusion evokes glances of suspicion. And what is the fourth and most important branch of government?

The fourth and most important branch of government is **the people themselves.** Of them is the origin of government. By them is the functioning of government. For them is the purpose of government. In the words of the immortal Lincoln, we are a "government of the people, by the people, and for the people." This is the only true and fundamental concept of constitutional government.

As STATED in the beginning of this article, it is extremely difficult to set down in capsule form the whole spectrum of human relationships. Yet, we realize more and more that people are so involved in the demands and ramifications of a complex society that they can't see the "forest because of the trees." In the throes of earning a living, of meeting the demands of ever increasing indebtedness and taxation, of trying to raise their offspring in an environment of exploding crime, it is little wonder that so many people are bewildered and unanchored as to their present, and future roles, in society. It has been our objective in these three articles to give perspective, establish new anchor points, and engender new hope for the future by having a clearer grasp of basic premises underlying all human relationships.

1. This planet of ours has provided an arena for performance of life within which both raw ingredients and levels of energy are sufficiently

abundant to provide the goods and wholesome life for each and every inhabitant.

2. No laws, institutions, or government can deny a solitary individual his inherent, or God-given right, of having access to the raw stock of Nature by either denying him the right of expending effort, or benefiting from accumulated know-how, in refining raw stock into usable products. It is the equal inherent right of every solitary individual to be a meaningful participant in society.

3. The people possess the full, and supreme, power to direct their lives as they envision and will their own future.

These are the premises, or yardsticks, by which we must analyze and evaluate existing ways of conducting the people's business. Such serious reflection will give us understanding of the extent to which financial, political and industrial oligopolies have flagrantly violated the rights of humans. Simultaneously we will commence to recognize the soundness and practicability of the Corporate Commonwealth approach as an economic and political framework in which individual rights are enhanced instead of destroyed.

Have we the will to act intelligently?

Liberty is every man's right to be himself within field of force that does not turn in on him and circumscribe him because it begins to injure or circumscribe others.

Nations-in-Law

William Dudley Pelley

~ 19 ~

Youth Replies, "I can!"

By William W. Pearson

*(The following speech, prepared by the son of the editors of **The Eagle's Eye**, was delivered by him at the Commencement Program for Noblesville High School, June 4, 1964 before a graduating class of 178 students. We present it herewith, with his permission, to indicate how some members of the younger generation view the future.)*

W HEN we, the graduating class of 1964, receive our diplomas tonight we will have reached one of the important milestones in our lives, but many others, more important, lie ahead.

High schools are always a time of growing up, of expectations often of rebellion. They are a time of inner questioning and outward pressures, of innumerable adjustments that are often painful. In addition, our generation confronts challenges and problems that no previous generation has ever had to face.

In three short years we will become of voting age, and we will have a legal voice in government. It is our duty to see that we are adequately prepared to vote intelligently and to voice our opinions clearly and firmly. Most important, it is imperative that we understand all problems and all challenges and prepare ourselves to think rationally and act forthrightly.

We have been faced with some of these problems all through high school, and others are materializing with each day that passes. They are problems of war and peace. They are problems of employment and unemployment, of automation and cybernation. They are problems of dropouts from school while knowledge is explosively expanding. They are problems of missiles and bombs that can accomplish total destruction. They are problems of bitter competition between men and between nations, of poverty and abundance.

None of these problems are Acts of God. They are manmade problems and as such, are solvable by man. The only question is whether we have the wisdom and the will to work out solutions. . . .

The Number One challenge today that must be understood and resolved concerns the decision between world peace and nuclear war. Never in the history of the world has man had the destructive power that he is now able to employ. The United States alone has a nuclear striking power equivalent to twenty tons of dynamite for every human being in the world. We have every reason to believe that Russia has the same. To unleash such tremendous destructive force can only mean the annihilation of all mankind. This means that nuclear weaponry has made war absolutely unthinkable.

We as rational people must somehow work out our differences with other nations of the earth so that nuclear holocaust can be deterred permanently. If we do not do so we will not have even the opportunity to work out the solutions to the other problems.

However, nuclear power does not have to be employed in making hydrogen bombs. It can be employed in providing unlimited energy to be harnessed for mankind's benefit.

The Second Challenge that must be faced is that of expanding Science and Technological Development. How we use this technological development will determine whether we are to be enslaved by machines, or whether we are to use these machines to erase poverty, illiteracy and disease from the surface of the globe.

Automation and cybernation, the ability of machines to perform all work automatically, are displacing millions of workers at a rapidly increasing rate. According to labor statistics, approximately 40,000 workers are thrown out of work each week.

Mr. Seymour Wolfbein, director of the Labor Department's Office of Manpower, Automations and Training has said, "The country will need twenty-two million more jobs by 1970 just to replace jobs lost through automation and higher productivity. To employ new workers joining the labor force will require twelve and one-half million additional jobs." Knowledgeable men in the field of cybernetic have testified to the fact that if all available technical knowledge and machinery were utilized, there would be need for only one-tenth of the current labor force, only 7,000,000 workers out of the 70,000,000.

Obviously it will be up to this generation to work out those adjustments in wages and hours that are necessary. And if they are justly worked out, with the full use of our technology, we shall not only begin to partake of the Horn of Plenty, but for the first time, we shall be able to work out constructive programs for the use of a new leisure.

This brings us to the Third Challenge, that of the explosion of Knowledge and the importance of education. In a basic sense, this challenge is the most vital for if it is met adequately, it will solve the other two. It is not generally realized that in the last ten years all knowledge has doubled since recorded history. Even more astounding is the fact that during the next three years all current knowledge will once again double.

It has been estimated that if a man, for example were to sit down and read all the material published this past year on scientific subjects, it would take 46 years just to read all of it. Every 24 hours, scientific material, equivalent to 168 volumes of the Encyclopedia Brittanica, is being written. Even with the tremendous assistance of computers and data-processing machines, it is quite obvious that no man can ever hope to learn everything.

Certainly those who unduly worry about leisure time have failed to grasp that education is a lifetime pursuit. They have failed to grasp the age of exploding knowledge that we have entered!

But assimilating knowledge means more than understanding our achievements in transportation, communication and productive potential. It should mean an understanding of man himself. Every individual must be given the opportunity to live a meaningful life. Freed from exacting labor and having leisure time, people will have greater opportunity to travel, to get to know the other people of the world and the lands, which they inhabit.

In years past, the people of one nation have been conditioned to hate the people of another, and without personal knowledge it was not difficult to picture them as devils that must be destroyed. Through our present exchange programs of students, scientists, athletes and entertainers, we are beginning to learn that people are all much alike over the earth wherever they may be found. These exchange programs, along with tourist travel, should be encouraged as much as possible. Increased knowledge and understanding between the peoples of all nations is the greatest step toward lasting world peace!

The importance of the youth of this generation cannot be overlooked. The world population is exploding so fast that at some time in this very decade, half the people of the world will be under 25 years of age. We are the heart of our nation's future. It is up to us to work out all problems, to accept all challenges and overcome them. The greater the challenge, the nobler the victory.

In the words of Ralph Waldo Emerson:

> *So nigh is grandeur of our dust,*
> *So near is God to man,*
> *When Duty whispers low, "Thou must!"*
> *The youth replies, "I can!"*

171

~ 20 ~

Integrity of the Individual

"The integrity of the individual must be preserved from the instant that he draws his first breath until the moment that he draws his last. That means it is the government's business to see that he does not die from hunger, any more than by lack of pure air, or by lack of water for his parched throat, or by the assassin's bullet.

Having established an order in which this is possible without beggaring anyone, that individual shall be enticed into personal achievement by having his willingness to work satisfied to the limit of his resources, health and ingenuity. He shall be allowed to acquire and retain all the personal property he is capable of earning and utilizing. He shall have full opportunity to show his mental or spiritual superiority over other men without exploiting them in the slightest because of their handicaps.

And most important of all, he shall not have coercive force above him in the form of a dictatorial group that styles itself a government merely because it has the force to preserve itself in power. The solid bloc of citizenry, enabled to express its will without red tape, bureaucracy or self-seeking officialdom, shall be the government, a true Republic really drawing its power from the consent of the governed, not a nominal republic so-called because once every two or four years the citizenry says who shall be the dictators to issue the arbitrary fiats.

No, this type of government has never been tried, but for that matter, neither has Christianity ever been tried!

Page 55, *No More Hunger*

172

~ 21 ~

"Absolute Power Corrupts Absolutely!"

ANY PERSON who makes a serious business of analyzing existing conditions is quick to discover a circumstance that permeates all levels of society. This circumstance is inescapably apparent irrespective of which facet of human relationships is to be considered. It is simply this: *There is one set of laws or code for moral behavior for those who possess power and there is another set and code for the majority who must move at the behest of those who administer that power.*

This double standard of both law and morality presents challenges that cannot be ignored by those who seek equity in all social structures.

Only the extremely naïve and gullible don't recognize the foregoing circumstance. Yet, such observation by the majority only encompasses a surface recognition. The average citizen is only aware if one has that money, plenty of that green stuff, or if one occupies high position in any power structure, or if one knows the right people, one can commit "murder" and get away with it.

On the other hand, if one is just an ordinary, struggling, tax-paying citizen, he can be sent to prison for merely stealing a five-gallon can of gasoline or failing to pay confiscatory taxes. However, the magnitude of the injustices and dangers inherent in all areas of concentrated power is beyond his knowledge.

IN 1959 a book was published entitled *Power and Morality*. Its authors were Pitirim Sorokin, Professor at Harvard, and Walter A. Lunden, Professor of Sociology at Iowa State University. The research for the book was supported by Mr. Lilly and the Lilly Endowment whose previous bequest had led to the establishment of the Harvard Research Center in Creative Altruism in 1949, which Professor Sorokin is now directing.

The important contribution that these distinguished professors have made, and it should be noted that both are learned men with many years of research and writing in the fields of sociology and criminality, is to historically substantiate Lord Acton's classic statement, "Power corrupts, and absolute power corrupts absolutely." Covering the past twenty-five centuries of Greco-Roman and Western civilization, they show that to the exact degree that power is exercised, to that same degree criminal behavior is present. The whole spectrum of crime, from bribery and fraud to killing and mass murder, is covered. No aspect, or level, of society is untainted by the corrupting influence of power.

Out of the whole research, which cites not only statistics of crime but relates them directly to persons and offices, emerges the irrefutable picture that the tendency toward crime are overwhelmingly more prevalent in those who *rule* than in the *ruled*.

Although increased power corrupts men, whether in industry, finance, or even in institutionalized religions,

174

the most naked and irresponsible display of power is in government themselves. Here we find that criminality has always exceeded that of the rank and file who have made up the citizenry. Every level of government is affected.

Whereas we readily associate brutality, chicanery and murder with pre-Western despotic rulers, most people are blind to the fact that outside of the larger part of the nineteenth century, when a reasonable degree of democratic participation existed both economically and politically, the nations of the world have reverted back to a condition of immorality and violence making the bestiality of the past insignificant by comparison.

In their introduction to "Power and Morality" the authors state, "Never before in history has the life or death of so many people depended upon so very few! The greatest autocrats of the past had but a fraction of the tremendous power held now by a few members of the Politbureau or the top leaders of the United States ruling elite. The dangerous situation naturally raises the momentous questions of our time: Can we entrust the fateful decision of war or peace, and through that the "life, liberty and pursuit of happiness" of hundreds of millions of human beings, to the few magnates of this power? Do they have the wisdom of the serpent and the innocence of the dove necessary to lead us to a lasting peace and a magnificent future?"

Authors Sorokin and Lunden answer their own questions by these succinct conclusions: "Still mainly tribal governments of politicians, by politicians, and for politicians, today's ruling groups, do not display the minimum of intellectual, moral and social qualifications necessary for a successful solution of these tremendous tasks. Throughout history the moral integrity of powerful governments has been, and still is, too low and their criminality too great to entrust to them the life and well being of mankind."

WE at Aquila are in accord with the basic thinking of the book *Power and Morality*. The authors have presented an historically supported thesis that "power corrupts, and absolute power corrupts absolutely." They also urgently plead for complete disarmament, fully recognizing the suicidal threat of thermonuclear holocaust, and logically urge the adoption of an "integral" order amongst mankind premised on love instead of hate.

Those of you who have read carefully what we have offered in all of our writings are aware that our chief emphasis has been on indicting systems *as* systems. We have stressed unequivocally that it is the very nature of Capitalism to concentrate power in fewer and fewer hands with larger and larger segments of the population denied both equity in and enjoyment of the nation's increased ability to produce all goods and services to abundance.

We have minced no words in labeling such a society a slave society with the spoils going to those who wield abnormal and abusive power!

Although it is specific individuals who exercise corrupt and criminal power, the basic wrong lies with the system, which permits and encourages the exercise of corruption and exploitation. Ultimately the whole society degenerates into an unstable condition with complete breakdown in the offing.

All levels of society have become victims. All are losers. The few have been corrupted by *over-participation*. The majority are increasingly driven to crime and immorality because of *under-participation*.

We have made a specific point of not over-concerning ourselves with indicting personalities. From the beginning we saw the folly and futility of concentrating on individuals or groups however criminal their actions. They appear and disappear with the passing of time but the faulty system persists through each succeeding generation. Our indictment must single out the social, economic and political arrangement itself, which methodically and diabolically makes criminals of all within its jurisdiction.

An analogy would be a car with a faulty steering mechanism. It should be apparent that whatever the skill of the driver, or his innate virtues, he would careen down the highway, endanger and take the lives of innocent persons, and inevitably end up in collision. Increase the horsepower of the engine and you simply compound the irresponsibility and criminal potential of the driver.

So it has been with the nation. Capitalism, camouflaged by such terms as "free enterprise" and "equal opportunity," has been a national vehicle without a constructively engineered steering mechanism. It has been a system, which gives privileged drivers the right to ride roughshod over anybody and everybody who questions or opposes oligarchic domination. It has been a system, which postulates that the ability to take advantage of people, to extort unearned tribute and to perpetuate war economies through unlimited sacrifice of American lives, carries with it the moral justification of all such dastardly acts.

How incredible that civilized man would have so long tolerated its existence!

HISTORICALLY, Capitalism got its impetus through private control of the nation's money supply, or credit, which automatically led to despotic commercial and political control. With no limitation on garnering the nation's resources and productive assets, it was just a matter of time before the whole economic structure functioned at the behest of an interrelated and interlocking directorate of monied and political power blocs.

The whole theory of a self-regulating market was but license for the shrewd and the unscrupulous to corral the real wealth of the nation. Despite the serious misgivings of the Founding Fathers, the Constitution had been adopted without any safeguards for the limiting of predatory power.

There is nothing sacred about Capitalism. Like Communism, it is a power-structure system and is unworkable. Neither system respects the dignity of the individual and his inherent right to be a sovereign participant in working out his well being. In both systems power begets power and with it progressive corruption. The only differentiation is that under Communism the political oligarchy runs the nation economically while under Capitalism the industrial-military and financial oligarchy runs the nation politically.

Both systems have double standards of morality and the administration of justice.

In our own nation nothing sickens the heart so much as to see the double standards of justice that maintain 'between those who wield power and the ordinary citizens. What justification exists in sending a boy of seventeen to prison for robbing the local filling station and imposing no restraint on monopolistic cartels that rob tens of millions of consumers every day through conspiratorial price-fixing? What justification exists, morally or ethically, for imprisoning the jobless father for holding up the local bank when that same bank is part of the usurious monetary structure that during the 1950's along "robbed" over $50,000,000,000 *(50 billion dollars!)* from the people in manipulated interest rates?

Certainly no one condones the taking of another's life. But we ask, what logic or code of morality upholds sending a young boy to prison for life because he commits murder and at the same time does not condemn and punish economic and political power blocs who are guilty of mass murder through promoted wars? Is murdur less murder because it is done in uniform or because the innocent women and children who are slaughtered are of a different skin-color?

Does the magnitude of criminal violence lessen guilt of the perpetrator? Or the fact that the triggering is done by governmental oligarchies instead of individuals?

THERE can be only one code of morality and one standard of justice for all people. This can only be achieved by making those who now wield abusive and criminal power to disgorge such immoral power. Recognizing that power corrupts both the few at the top and the majority at the bottom, the only hope for humanity lies in dispersing power back to the hands of all the people where it inherently belongs. When this happens, for the first time not only will corruption disappear along with all forms of violence, but man's latent love emotion will have the opportunity of displaying itself.

Belatedly people must recognize that the power criminally exercised by the oligarchic blocs in our society was acquired by disadvantaging and exploiting all the people. Therefore restoration of the power to the people, and a restoration of the nation's resources and technology to all the people, can be done morally and legally. All that is necessary is sufficient public enlightenment to take the necessary steps.

We at Aquila have advanced the idea of a "Cooperative Commonwealth" because within this framework there would exist an equilibrium of holdings and the people themselves would exercise absolute power in democratically working out all material needs. No individual would be excluded and yet a negotiated gradient scale would determine incomes above the guaranteed basic-necessity income of every citizen. Under a corporate arrangement, where all citizens were the stockholders, the maximum good life could be enjoyed directly commensurate with our maximum ability to produce everything.

Politically, it must come to pass that the people express the final voice on all major legislation and policy, especially that of war. With the perfecting of instant communications, so that there can be constant and full televised coverage of all issues being debated, there is no reason why the people should not vote and make the final decision on all proposed legislation affecting them.

To leave political power in the hands of the few is to invite corruption and misuse of authority. History has given us an overwhelming lesson and the price has been too high to be tolerated.

Of course none of these basic reforms can come about if mass violence in the form of war cannot be brought to an abrupt halt. Nuclear weaponry now exists in the hands of power oligarchies, both in this nation and the world, which could obliterate the planet and annihilate mankind. Every voice must plead for negotiations and for complete disarmament.

A sane society and a peaceful world *are* attainable. It is only a question whether or not sufficient people have the will to live in a world of lasting peace and justice for all!

At Last!

THE BOOK THAT HAS THE ANSWER

To the Employment Problem – to the Farm Problem – to the Mortgage Problem – to the Crime Problem – to the Housing Problem and above all *to the Attainment of Peace*

"NO MORE HUNGER"
By William Dudley Pelley

YOU WILLL ENVISION how all our resources, manpower and best technological know-how can be utilized in providing for not only the people's material needs abundantly, but also for full educational, cultural and medical facilities available for every citizen.

YOU WILL RECOGNIZE the fallacious premise of the so-called "profit" system and all forms of usury and mortgages, which have regimented an entire nation into bondage.

YOU WILL GAIN perspective of the true role of a sovereign people constantly directing government as servant and not bureaucratic overlord.

ABOVE ALL you will have faith in knowing that you can join with others in striving for goals that are attainable!

~ 23 ~

"Spiral Downward into Oblivion"

Whereas many people are well aware of the horrifying destructive power of nuclear weaponry, few are the people who are aware of the fact that increased nuclear build-up in armaments seriously lessen our survival potential. What they fail to recognize is that a point in military history has been passed where our national security decreases in direct ratio to an increase in military power. This seeming paradox was clearly brought out by two of the nation's leading scientists in the current *Scientific American*.

In a joint article by Dr. Jerome B. Weisner and by Dr. Herbert F. York they state, "the clearly predictable course of the arms race is a steady open spiral downward into oblivion." Weisner is Dean of Massachusetts Institute of Technology, after serving as science advisor to President Kennedy. Dr. York is Chancellor of the University of California and was chief scientist in the Defence Department's Advanced Research Project's Agency in the Eisenhower Administration.

These two skilled scientists emphasized the circumstance that neither the United states nor Russia can hope to achieve a decisive military advantage, offensively or defensively, through future military research. "Ever since shortly after World War II," they wrote,

183

"the military power of the U. S. has been rapidly and inexorably diminishing."

The authors added further, "From the Soviet point of view, the picture is similar but much worse. The military power of the USSR has been steadily increasing since it became an atomic power in 1949. Soviet national security, however, has been steadily decreasing. Hypothetically, the United States could decide to destroy the USSR and the USSR would be absolutely powerless to prevent it. That country could only, at best, seek to wreak revenge through whatever retaliatory capability it might then have left."

It us our considered professional judgment that this dilemma has no technical solution. So stated Dr. Weisner and Dr. York. Their judgment leaves no other alternative but complete disarmament. They cited the Nuclear Test Ban Treaty as an important step toward finding a multilateral solution and pleaded for additional steps leading to meaningful peace.

THE SIGNIFICANCE of the article by two of the nation's most responsible scientists must not escape our thinking. Too many Americans have smugly measured our security by the increased perfecting of our nuclear weaponry. Just the reverse has happened. As we have made bigger bombs, and improved our delivery systems, this has forced the Russians to do likewise. And the same has held true regarding our response to an ever-increasing capability by the Russians. War technology has actually decreased the security of both nations.

This then is the dilemma that faces not only Russia and the United States, but the whole world. There can be no victors in modern warfare. The nations of the world are hell-bent on a path of destruction in which their best technology and human resources are employed for the ultimate annihilation of mankind instead of creating a social environment wherein all such hardships as disease and drudgery and chronic poverty are eliminated that have plagued and warped so many hundreds of millions. A realistic acceptance of at least temporary co-existence and a just and effective negoiating of our differences must come to pass. Blackened corpses strewn across the international landscape will only give mute testimony to people who had lost all reverence for life itself.

But it is not enough simply to plead with the average American to raise his voice and demand a cessation to unclear build-up, to call for a return of American boys from the undeclared war in Viet Nam, and to plead for bigger and bigger Geneva get-togethers. All these approaches can only serve to stave off imminent disaster. They are not permanent solutions. However, they are necessary steps that mankind may have a breathing spell in which to get at the basic causes of wars. The real motivations for wars are considerably deeper.

Clear in people's thinking must be the recognition that the privileged power-blocks in our capitalistic society, the same as the abnormal forces in the communistic society, have economic and political stakes in "cold" and " hot" wars. This is not to say that there isn't genuine worldwide contest between these two major systems contending for domination. It is stating that systems as systems are advancing regimentation of their respective citizenry through global confrontations that have nothing to do with people as people. It is important that we make this distinction.

The people of Russia have no more hatred for the American people than we have for the Russians. Both nations are composed of tens of millions of quite ordinary citizens who seek only the opportunity to live decently and with dignity. In turn they seek this environment for their children. Unfortunately, neither capitalism nor communism affords this for the vast majority. What hypocrisy that the lives of so many hundreds of millions on both sides can be pitted in a life-and-death struggle to destroy each other over systems whose objectives in war are never fulfilled in peace!

A nation's foreign policy can never exceed in integrity that of its national policy. Only if, and when, the peoples of all countries put their own houses in order will wars, and threats of wars, vanish from the earth. A people enjoying the full increment of their labor and resources need not impose their way of life on others by force. It is embraced by demonstrable example. This should be America's true role!

~ 24 ~

Your Stake in a Bountiful Universe! . . .

IN THE September issue we stated that the average American is confused and bewildered as to his rightful role in society. He is at a loss as to what he should think or what he should do. Further and further he drifts into apathy and displays an indifference as to the future of his nation. Instead of confronting problems and intelligently protesting existing injustice, he tries to escape from cruel reality. At the other end of the social spectrum are the lesser number who are openly rebelling against a society that has not provided them with meaningful roles. Both reactions are the products of an irrational environment within which human rights are flagrantly ignored and violated.

It is the feeling of Aquila that the national house will never be put in order by a blind reliance on politicians who are but the spokesmen of the monied power-blocks that are responsible for the disorder in the first place. Ultimately, it must be the people themselves who effect their own deliverance from predatory interests by fully understanding the causes of their basic problems. Thus, the whole hope for a renovated America becomes one of education. A people who want to be free must be aroused to want to live decently and wholesomely, and without the burdens of needless indebtedness.

There is no magic wand that can be waved that will automatically enlighten the people. Nor can a people filled with despair be condemned for their lack of initiative in seeking a way out from their troubles. People must be accepted exactly as they are with full recognition that they are basically good, that they would properly indict wrongdoing, and that they would embrace corrective measures if they had the yardsticks with which to measure the worth of the laws, institutions, and economic systems. It is with this thought in mind that we decided to devote the next three magazines to main articles dealing with cardinal premises underlying all human relationships.

The first premise is that **we live in a good and rational Universe.** Many may wonder what bearing this consideration has on earning a living, paying bills and educating children. The thought might even be entertained that such topic is more befitting a discussion in astronomy than economics or politics. Such hasty conclusion, however, is without merit. There is a vitally important lesson to be learned when each person gets the full impact that he or she is an inherent stockholder in a rational Universe, and is an equal owner of all raw stock simply by being born.

How often do we hear someone exclaim, "What a cruel world we live in!" Granted such outcry stems from sheer frustration of eking out an existence, or the loss of home by foreclosure, or even a loved one apprehended in crime, it is nonetheless true that many people do attribute life's trials and tribulations to a vengeful God or a Universe that is too demanding. To whatever exent such thinking exists, we want no part of it. It is blasphemy against a Creator that has displayed overwhelming benevolence and rationality in

His endowments to all mankind. It is Man himself that has turned a potential Paradise into a land where want and hardship abound needlessly.

The important thought to guide your thinking is that man arrived on this planet and found all raw stock, including untapped energies, waiting for him. He didn't arrive with even as much as a toothbrush. Nor did he arrive with any gilt-edged charter, carrying a divine seal, which designated a certain allotment of raw ingredients to one person, a smaller portion to another, and failed to make provisions for the vast majority. Since no one arrives with any bag of raw stock, and since no divine apportionments divides natural resources, it has to be concluded that each person born has equal right to the Creator's beneficence. There are no favorites. No one has any right to create such circumstance as excludes others from equal enjoyment of all that Nature has provided.

IT IS HIGHLY important that each person recognizes that there is not one product that can be made without using some part of Nature herself. This includes more than the trees, the water, the minerals, the soil and the air we breathe. It includes the most basic elements composing matter and all levels of energy that are released in both fission and fusion. Everything outside of Man is the material, the building blocks, of Nature and no one has priority in their ownership. They belong to each and every person born into existence.

It is in the light of the foregoing that we can evaluate the injustice of men, or institutions, or economic arrangements that succeed in building fences around the major portions of natural wealth and prevent tens of

189

millions of people from expending their own effort in refining raw stock into needed products to sustain life. What of the rights of the newborn child who comes into life and finds that monopolists and financial manipulators have excluded him even before he arrived? Isn't monopoly of natural resources a double crime against humanity when it can be perpetuated against oncoming generations through unearned inheritance?

Doesn't the same hold true in respect to all knowledge that has been accumulated up the centuries? Why hasn't the newborn baby, irrespective of parents or place of birth, just as much right to the contributions of the Newtons, the Wattses, the Bells, the Faradays, the Edisons, the Enrico Fermis, to all the advancements in communications, transportations and productive technology, as any of the ruthless monopolists that have corralled the nation's assets? What unwritten law gives the private banking fraternity, and the industrial-military complex exclusive right to the vast reservoir of knowledge, which is a legacy of the people? Isn't it simply because monied interests have taken over the whole economy, dominate with despotic control, and can arbitrarily exclude the people from enjoying all the science that is the people's heritage?

A confused and apathetic people must awaken to the gross injustice that is meted out to them and to their children. They must awaken to the fact that their stake in this nation far exceeds any of the "paper" ownership of usurers and property barons. It exceeds a thousand-fold the most important scientific breakthrough by any one person in one lifetime. Their claim is based not only on all existing resources but also on all the genius and labor that underlies the advancement of man since the planet was first inhabited.

This also includes current technology, the nation's present productive potential, which has been developed and expanded for the most part through "administered prices" paid by the nation's consumers, and scientific research underwritten by the nation's taxpayers. It is absurd and invalid to contend that a handful of major stockholders are the *only rightful owners* of our vast productive machinery. *All* the people have made it possible.

WE ARE NOT making any plea for the sharing alike of all goods and services, irrespective of the amount of labor put forth by each individual, although we have crossed the threshold into an era of cybernation, the science of skilled-machines operating skilled-machines, in which it will become increasingly difficult to translate each person's rightful claim based solely on wages. Under a New Order of economic structure, directed and controlled democratically by a sovereign people, only a minimum of a labor force will be needed to fill to abundance all needs of all people.

The important thing to appreciate is that neither earning power, nor capability of parents, should be the basis for determining the claim of each child to full education and a material stake in the nation. At the same time it should be clear in our thinking that full enjoyment of life by the elderly is not a matter of charity but should be based on earned and *inherent* credit against which to draw for the remainder of their years. We should make it fundamental in our thinking that all people, from the lowliest of citizens to the most avaricious at the top, have equal *inherent* credit.

Yes, this is a Good Universe that we occupy. It is more than lush with an abundance of raw stock to fashion the answer to man's every necessity. It is a source of unlimited energy simply awaiting release so that every burden of hard labor can be lifted from man's back. It is impartial to all men and displays balance and rationality in all its movements. It is man that displays waste of energy, waste of movement, and waste of matter. It is man's arrogant belief that he can violate the laws of Nature and suffer no consequences.

The forces that have enslaved mankind know that their Rigged Game is up the moment a sovereign people recognize that the Universe was not brought into existence in order that a handful of the strongest and most unscrupulous might peonize the rest of humanity. Not only are all resources the rightful property of all the people, as well as all the contributions of history, but within the earthly arena every human being has inherent rights that are entitled to full and individual expression.

A people who want to be free must recognize their rightful heritage in the whole Universe. It is such identity with the Creator Himself that restores ballast to people's thinking and gives them a solid position from which to challenge the forces that have denied so many millions their birthright. It is wishful thinking to believe that abnormal power-blocks in our society will relinquish without a struggle. Yet relinquish they must when the might of an awakened citizenry demands its own deliverance.

In succeeding issues we will cover the specific innate rights of every human being, and the supreme power of the people to make all changes. Until then imbed in

192

your consciousness and your mind that every solitary human being has a stake in a Good and Rational Universe. To deny it is to deny your own birthright!

~ 25 ~

"We, *the People,* of the United States . . "

IN the last issue of *The Eagle's Eye* we covered briefly the three major areas in which the large power structures despotically dominate in this nation. We listed them as political control, monetary control and productive control. The crux of what we presented was that until such control is restored to the sovereign people there could be no realistic solving of the nation's problems.

There is little doubt in our minds that most of the readers, along with the majority of the people throughout the land, are quite aware that all is not what it should be in any of the three areas bearing on the life of all citizens. The sham and hypocrisy of national conventions, the high interest charges and foreclosures of private banking, and the price-fixing of monopolists and the wholesale exit of the small businesses, all these are obvious evidences of the dishonesty and inequity that exist in these areas.

We are also aware that details of how monopolistic control disservices the majority only stress to the reader what is already evident. In short, it is quite apparent to all that much is wrong. However, when we advance solutions to the major problems, we encounter the unwillingness of too many people to let go of the old methods and embrace the new.

Consequently, we have the ironical circumstance of a people not wanting to be slaves but at the same time fearing to break the shackles that enforce their servitude.

Of course, this isn't the full picture. People have been so long restrained in eking out an existence, and have so long had dinned in their ears the "idealisms" of the past, that new methods pose a picture of stepping into unchartered territory without adequate assurance of success. It is all a proposition of fearing that which one doesn't fully understand.

I T IS in view of the foregoing that we have decided to devote the next three issues to taking up separately the three areas we have referred to and see if we can't increase our understanding of what the new methods or reforms would encompass. As we do, it will be unmistakably apparent to each that what is advocated can all be done within the framework of the Constitution. In fact, what changes we advocate would put new life into that document and give strength to the fulfillment of its intent.

This issue will take up the need of a people to exercise meaningfully their political sovereignty. Stated in its most basic sense, we are considering *the inherent right of every solitary individual to have a voice in the making of all laws and policies that governs his conduct and which bear on his survival and well being.* It is the purpose of our presentation to give some thought first to the inherent and supreme power of the people themselves, and then devote the balance of the article to showing the feasibility of such exercise of power in light of modern technology.

Earlier we spoke of old methods and the difficulty for people to embrace new approaches. In no area of American life does this barrier persist so tenaciously as in our political life. Yet it is in this area that the nation's health and security must be worked out. It is in this area that the people who have the absolute power to do *anything* and *everything* toward commanding their maximum well being have been shorn of that power. They have been tricked into belief that the power really does not belong to them.

The people have been led to accept that the methods of exercising political decision of the past are the only correct methods. Somehow it is contended that if you do a thing wrong long enough it becomes correct. Students of popular government have recognized that all such persuasion is only for the gullible and unthinking.

They have recognized that usurpation of the people's sovereign power has been achieved because the people have not only given the right *to select* their candidates to political machines, but they have given such power-bloc candidates, when elected, the unlimited power *to act* independent of the interests or wishes of the people.

Deception of Two-party System

FIRST, let us consider this holier-than-holy concept of the present so-called "two-party" system. To hear the proponents, and apologists, defend such system, one would think that the whole idea had been delivered to this nation on tablets of gold by angelic messenger. In fact, anyone brash enough to question its divine validity is quickly charged with blaspheming the Almighty and promoting anarchy. It is all a ruse to protect the usurpers of authority.

Of course the defender of the two major political parties will offer plausible reasons for their existence. He will tell you that they make possible divergent points of view and thus the electorate has a choice in voting for candidates. Theoretically, this seems convincing. In practice, it is quite different. Such theory is but a smokescreen blinding the people to the irrefutable fact that both candidates are selected by the multi-million dollar machines that are but the front men for the other power structures in our society. Even on the local level the local "establishment" exercises the prevailing voice.

More serious, of course, is the development that the elected candidate has assumed no obligation to speak for the people but is beholden to those who nominated him and underwrote his campaign. Political parties, as they function in this nation, are interlocking monopolies with the commands at the top sifting down to the lowliest precinct.

Payola of Patronage

The glue that holds the whole conglomerate of usurpation together is *patronage*. From the operating of the local license bureau by the County Chairman to the appointing of Federal postmasters, to the recommending of judgeships, to the awarding of hundreds of billions of tax-dollars in war contracts, both political parties employ patronage to perpetuate their existence through enforced allegiance.

The result is that elected candidates are in the business of making political "pay-offs" and not in the

197

business of reflecting the rights and interests of the people. What a hollow mockery has been made of the people's political sovereignty and their inherent right to have a participating voice in passing, and changing, all laws and policies governing their conduct.

ULTIMATELY, the people will secure a constitutional amendment that will outlaw not only the two-party system but all political parties. The supreme power of the people cannot find expression through mechanisms, which are designed to adulterate the direct wishes of the people. A people who want to make any steps toward liberating themselves from the oligarchic domination of private banking and the industrial-military complex must first recognize the need to effect their political liberation.

To those who might be disconcerted at the thought of no political parties, let it quickly be added that in actuality there would be *one political party* and that would be the *people themselves*. In fact, it has always existed, but has lain dormant, permitting artificial entities to usurp or misdirect its power.

It is significant too note that the Founding Fathers in writing the Constitution didn't commence by stating that "We, the Democrats," or "We, the Republicans," or "We, the private bankers," or "We, the military-industrial complex of the United States in order to form a more perfect union . . ." but declared, "We, *the people* of the United States . . ." It was the professional politicians that came later who advanced the unfounded concept that the people are too dumb to rule and any decision-making power exercised by the people is tantamount to "mob rule" or "putting mediocrity on a pedestal." Supinely the people have accepted such degrading of their own power and collective wisdom and left "life, liberty and happiness" to professional politicians. The kind of a nation and the kind of world we have today is living testimony to the people's own dereliction of responsibility.

It must be recognized that geographical barriers did exist at the inception of this nation that required the delegating of power by the people to representatives. In this era of advanced technology in instant communication, verbally and pictorially, there is no necessity for such delegation. For the first time, the tools exist by which the sovereign people can retain the full power, the exclusive power of decision-making.

Candidates of the People

The first step is to recognize that all candidates must be candidates of the people. From every practical and honest approach, this is what is done today. If a number of people want a candidate who will directly reflect the wishes of his constituency, they seek out an independent candidate, one who is free from the payola of party politics. Of course, he seldom gets elected because the deciding factor is not his qualification but the amount of campaign finances available.

It is in light of this circumstance, if none other, that presentation of candidates to the electorate should be a function of society itself. The only requirement for a person desiring political office should be that he can obtain a reasonably determined number of voters vouching for his candidacy. Then every candidate should have an equal opportunity to present himself to his electorate. It is the far-reaching potential of television that makes this possible and meaningful.

To a large degree, presentation of candidates on local or national TV is done today. It is now possible to bring every candidate into the living room of every citizen. In the case of those not having television sets, public places could be designated so that no one would be excluded from being informed. But it isn't only the candidate, or even the elected official, that should be intimately presented. The functioning of every level of government should be televised on one duly assigned channel so that the citizenry have a constant opportunity to observe what their elected representatives are doing.

Making it possible for any citizen to be a candidate for office, free from the dictates and dependency of political parties, and giving him equal opportunity to present his qualifications and platform, plus televising government in action, could be immediate realizations. But this is only a feeble first step compared to what could be done in permitting every person to become truly a participating and decision-making citizen.

Democracy in Action

Under a Cooperative Commonwealth, within which our best technology would be used, full democracy in action could be a practical reality. Through the use of television in conjunction with the computerized telephone, all voting and decision-making could be done directly from the home. David Sarnoff, Chairman of the Board of Radio Corporation of America in an address made last year, directed the following remarks on the technical potential of the foregoing:

"Balloting would take place within a specified time period, at the voter's convenience. The individual would set his television receiver to a special voting channel and view a demonstration of the procedure to be followed. He would then identify himself over the telephone by transmitting his personal code number to the regional computer. This would be verified in the computer memory, along with his eligibility, before a pushbutton vote could be cast, and there would be built-in safeguards against voting frauds.

"Within minutes after closing time the regional computers would forward the data to national computers serving as central tabulators, and results would be announced less than an hour after the closing of the home polls. At the same time, the computer would provide detailed analyses of the election for use on the airways and in the press. By these means, it could be possible to achieve an almost total expression of the popular will by those qualified to vote.

"In a democratic society, other significant possibilities are inherent in such a system. For example, a computerized process similar to that used in home voting could obtain a prompt expression of public opinion on a wide range of issues. We could have national, regional or local plebiscites on anything from a proposed municipal tax to a contemplated change in the latest model car."

The People Supreme

It is in light of the foregoing technical ability of the citizenry to constantly direct and run their own government and formulate their own policies that we want to stress the major innovation that must ultimately be embraced if the people are to be truly sovereign. It is this:

The inherent power of the people should be exercised directly and absolutely in the passage of all legislation and in the adoption of all major policy.

This would be the culmination of a true democratic society. For the first time the people themselves would be arbiters of their own well-being and destiny. Government of the people, by the people, and for the people would have become a dynamic actuality and not just an "idealism" to which politicians give lip service.

In practical operation, what would such majority-rule government provide? Would it mean, as some fear, that the most intelligent in our midst would be excluded from affording the nation the benefit of their greater knowledge and skills? By no means. In fact, a political environment would exist within which the most intelligent could play roles devoid of the pressures of the unscrupulous and predatory in society.

Mark this important contrast. Whereas candidates for office are now dependent for their reelection on the political machines, and thereby must do their bidding, under a circumstance where the people ruled supreme the candidates would be directly responsible to the people. All public offices would attract only those who were motivated to serve the betterment of society.

The real safeguard would be, of course, in the final decision-making prerogative exercised by the people. The most intelligent and qualified would be elected to office for the purpose of *recommending* legislation and policy. They would perform the role of researching and debating the needs of the nation.

Then, at an appropriate time all their findings would be presented to the people, along with their legislative proposals. The *final judgment, or decision,* would be made by the sovereign people.

The lessons of history have been cruel and exacting, in both treasure and blood, when people have delegated to others the unchecked power to make all decisions. Overwhelmingly, it is borne out that tendencies to criminality and corruption are more evident in the rulers than in those ruled.

The greatest distortion and fiction of history has been the calculated propaganda that majority rule must be equated with mob rule. Those who have always sought to disadvantage the people have known that while the few can be corrupted, it is impossible to corrupt the majority. Fully informed people voting in self-interest will display rationality and justice.

No society, considering those where a reasonable amount of education is available, can reach any heights of morality and material blessings until power has its widest dispersal. Under a Cooperative Commonwealth where every citizen has a shareholding voice, there would be fulfillment of the bedrock axiom, "Out of the greatest participation comes the greatest good."

Until such New Order in human relationships comes about the guideline for each of us is to give recognition to, and work through, the one and only valid political party, *the people themselves.*

~ 26 ~

Thanksgiving --- 1964

ON THIS Holy Day of giving gratitude unto Thee for those many blessings which the brethren without the Enlightenment fail to acknowledge.

We thank Thee for the celestial gift of Consciousness, by which we Know Ourselves and exert the faculties of Reason.

We thank Thee for the wonder of Elective Mortality that gives us sensations of Pain and Pleasure, by which Intellect is wrought and Knowledge becomes our birthright.

We thank Thee for the gift of Hard Experience with difficulties, distresses, quandaries, ordeals, that leave us prostrate of physical strength, that we may know the joys or energy's renewal and the stamina to persist when the weakling wail and leave us.

We thank Thee for Error that by its evils Truth stands clear to us; for Deceit and False Doctrine, that by its deployments we recognize Wisdom; for Darkness that we sing when Light breaks upon us.

We thank Thee for bad government in this land of our Fathers, that we, the children, awaken to its evils and establish the Righteous.

We thank Thee for Hatred that we may learn love; for War, that by our high efforts we bring in Tranquility.

We thank Thee for Storm, and Ruin, and Privation and Hunger, that we may grow the strength equal to every complication, that our souls become malleable with mettle of Nobilities, that we walk without Fear on the Shining Uplands of Divinity, Ladies and Gentlemen whose hearts cannot be vanquished.

For these, on this Thanksgiving, we thank Thee!

William Dudley Pelley

VALOR , November 22, 1952

~ 27 ~

"Not One Cent for Tribute!"

ONCE AGAIN the deadline approaches for the annual tax report on the incomes of the American people. The deadline of April 15th not only covers the Federal tax but in many states includes the tax on gross earnings. This is the time of year when gripes over the high cost of operating government are the loudest and most frequent. However, few get the full impact of the whole labyrinthine tax structure for what it is, a colossus of "taxation without representation." Instead it is accepted as a necessary "adjunct" of democracy, granting, of course, that there are inequities.

To most citizens, income tax reports have become just an annoying routine, a time for filing forms. In most cases there is no need even to remit actual cash. The employer as tax collector has withheld each week sufficient amounts to cover all tax liabilities. Perhaps a passing glance at his W-2 form gives the taxpayer a momentary jolt when he sees the total taxes he has paid for the purported purpose of operating his government. But that's about the extent of his reaction. In fact his employer has already been deducting from his wages for three months in this year 1964 and he hasn't really missed such deductions. Increasing property taxes resulting in direct burdens and foreclosures are another story.

To the serious-minded citizen, to the person who can reason from cause to effect, and who wants to do something to put his nation on stable keel, the whole tax structure shapes up as quite something else. Considering the literally hundreds of billions of dollars that have been squandered around the globe and wasted at home, the whole process of taxation has not been far short of legalized extortion for the perpetuation of irresponsible politicians, beholden to monied forces and not the people.

No one should object to paying his share of the legitamate expenses of operating government and the underwriting of necessary public services. But every red-blooded citizen should vehemently protest the paying of a *tribute* to overlords for the sole "privilege" of being their vassal.

Across the land must ring out the stirring admonition of the Founding Fathers, "Millions for defense (our well-being), but not one cent for tribute!" Tribute comes from servants or slaves. It is the government that is set up to be the servant of the people. To be otherwise nullifies its role as government. It then becomes despotism.

Please bear in mind that two ingredients must always be present if a society is to be free. First, the people must be informed. Secondly, government must at all times function within the scope of powers delegated to it by the people.

LET us briefly consider the current 11.5 billion dollar tax cut, which has been given so much publicity. Even just a cursory analysis bears out that the whole package is but a political sedative to quiet the more restless of the citizenry. First, observation is that the tax reduction has no bearing on the lowest income groups in the nation simply because they do not have large enough incomes to be taxed in the first place. Yet, here is where the most needed relief should be focused. These are the one-fifth of our nation who are in need of food, clothing and adequate housing.

How about the five million unemployed? How does the tax reduction affect wages they don't even get? When you consider the income groups of four, five and six thousand dollars per year, the salary groups who would immediately spend any increased income, you find that their increase is practically negligible. It is those on the higher brackets who get the bigger tax reductions, and these people don't need the money for necessities, but are the ones most apt to invest such savings in tax-exempt government bonds. Unfortunately, the 38 million in poverty, the unemployed, and the workers in the lower brackets are left out of the picture.

Consider now the absurdity of the tax reductions for the larger corporations. What logical reason can be given for the proposition that tax savings will permit further expansion of plant capacity and therefore more jobs will be available? Already a large percentage of productive machinery is standing idle in every major industry. Does more idle machinery put more men to work? In fact, since almost all plant investments are presently allocated for the installing of automated equipment, expansion of industry through any corporation tax cuts can only mean fewer workers than currently employed. Automated machinery displaces men; it does not provide for additional employment. Less men working means less purchasing power to buy the increased goods produced by automated industry.

This is the alarming prospect that the nation faces during this decade. There will be ever-increasing *surplus men* vainly trying to acquire ever-increasing *surplus products*. Is it difficult to see that this is the perfect setting for government to step in with its demands for increased taxes, invariably accompanied with overbearing bureaucracy and despotic regimentation?

One would have to be shallow-minded to view the tax-cut as anything other than a token gesture, pitiful at that, in restoring the destroyed purchasing power of the people. Along with the current proposed 962 million dollar "attack" on poverty, the tax-reduction bill is more a political expedient than any solid move to offer relief or put our economy in order. Politicians are primarily interested in votes, not solutions making their constituents independent and not in need of demagogues.

Underneath the whole economic terrain the major "faults" are widening. The rumblings and pressures are becoming louder and greater. When and how human eruptions will come about as oppression breaks its chains, we can only speculate. That they will happen there can be no question.

No PERSON can make a study of the whole tax structure without being appalled at the fact that in the final analysis the only persons who pay taxes are the tens of millions of citizens in this nation who are the bulk of wage earners and consumers. No one else really pays taxes. To conclude, or accept, that corporations, or the large income groups, pay taxes is to deal in fantasy. Such conclusions or acceptances are myths and are devoid of realism.

The Barry Goldwaters and Liberty Amendment advocates should awaken to the fact that the progressive income tax is not in need of being abolished. Above a certain level it no longer exists. Studies reveal that actually as incomes increase, the amount of taxes paid decreases. That is in the highest brackets of income. A lot of complacent Americans should be shocked to learn that none of the so-called rich pay anything like the supposed 91% tax. In fact, many of the million-a-year men pay no tax at all. And these, who do pay, pay proportionately less than those in the lower brackets.

In an article appearing recently in the *Saturday Evening Post,* written by Stewart Alsop, and which he claimed was based on statistics prepared by the Office of Tax Analysis of the Office of the Secretary of the Treasury, some most revealing facts were brought to the light of day. It was stressed that the statistics used applied to typical taxpayers and not special tax situations. The first shocker was the fact that a person with a million-dollar income paid only about 26% on his adjusted gross income of a million dollars. And even this was not an accurate percent of his real income since so much of wealthy men's money is in tax-free bonds, the income from which need not be reported to the Treasury.

Further, it came to light that according to the Treasury analysis there were 20 very rich people who paid no income tax at all. Three persons in the $500,000 to $750,000 a year group paid no taxes. Of the nineteen Americans with incomes of more than 5 million dollars per year, five, or more than 25%, paid no tax at all. Twelve of them paid less than 50%. It is brazen deception to contend that the rich pay through the nose in taxes. And by the way, what human is worth $5,000.000 a year? . . .

WHAT must be realized is that the people with more money than they can use, or are worth, can afford to hire high-priced attorneys who are not only unscrupulous but are most adept at locating the loopholes in the tax structure. Every sort of technique is resorted to in order to keep from paying taxes, capital gains, depletion allowances for oil and other resources, real-estate deals, charity, tax-free bonds. And if such "evasions" do not suffice, there is simply failure to file returns, with later settlements if caught. The latter include such publicly "esteemed" personalities as Judge Landis, one-time dean of the Harvard Law School, who received a hand-slap for having failed to file income reports for a number of years.

When we come to corporations, especially the giant monopolies, we have to consider tax-exempt foundations and charitable trusts. These number some 45,000. The foundations range from the giants set up by the Ford and Rockefeller families to small charitable outfits organized by affluent individuals and corporations. In October 1963, a report was released by a subcommittee, headed by Wright Patman, on the "Economic Impact of Foundations and Trusts." In the last 11 years, said the Patman report, only 113 foundations had been audited by the Internal Revenue Service. When it comes to supervising foundations, the report concluded, " the IRS record is a dud, a dismal failure."

The Patman report went on to state, "the use of foundations for business devices and for tax avoidance has become a major economic evil and must be stopped.

Otherwise we will degenerate into a nation with one law for the rich and another law for the poor." At another point, the report said, "the Treasury prefers to remain arrogantly ignorant of the enormous concentration of economic power among foundations." The 534 foundations studied by the subcommittee had assets exceeding $7,000,000,000 (*7 billion dollars!*). They had stock in 2000 corporations.

It should be borne in mind that when foundations set up to escape taxes by the large corporations, there is a "legal" aspect for so doing. But how many taxpayers give thought to the fact that monopolistic corporations by their very power to administer prices have to all intents and purposes usurped a power "to tax" all consumers. Included in the selling price of their produce is not only a complete coverage of all costs of manufacture, overhead, and exorbitant executive salaries, but reserves for expansion, plus absorption of all tax liabilities. While the government may tax the corporation, it in turn simply passes the tax down to the consumer.

Contrast this with the wage-earner, or retired person, who cannot pass the tax down to anyone but must sacrifice living standards, too often bare necessities, in order to absorb the rich man's tax. Such injustice, multiplied by the tens of millions of American workers and consumers, would ignite an open revolution overnight if the victims en masse grasped the wholesale inequity of the power *to tax* by non-government forces.

On FEBRUARY 25, 1913, the 16th Amendment to the Constitution was adopted which made the Income Tax the law of the land. Many who recognize the inequities of this amendment, especially in its execution, are blind to the fact that a far greater miscarriage of equity came into being that same year in the passage of the Federal Reserve Act. In the one instance the government was given the power to extract "tributes" from all citizens that political machines could be perpetuated. In the second instance, privately owned corporations, or banks, were given the power to extract "tributes" in the form of interest, and were given the diabolical power to debase, or devalue, the currency and purchasing power of all the people. In the latter case we have a clear usurpation of power that belongs inviolately to the government, meaning the people themselves.

No greater, over-all crime has been perpetrated against the American people, or any people for that matter, than the issuance and manipulation of their nation's money and credit. It is more than the power to tax and even confiscate property. It is the power to enslave!

FROM the beginning the whole tax structure was earmarked for eventual failure. It has far outlived its value, is archaic and cumbersome, and is unjust, in this age of streamlined, jet-speed production and communication. Equally obsolete and unjust is the whole structure and approach of our dog-eat-dog competition with all the spoils, or profits, going to the biggest accumulators of power, even if tens of millions are hungry and in want. Deb-money manipulations by private usurers must be even more strongly condemned as incompatible with a free society.

As a people who wish to be free and prosper, we must have the courage to take stock of the structural faults of capitalism, retaining those aspects which are constructive and embracing new approaches where necessary. We need not concern ourselves with personalities or name-calling. The crisis is too large for that. We must concern ourselves with remedial reform simply as to its fairness and workability.

Under a Corporate Commonwealth, as presented in *No More Hunger,* taxes, as they are today, would be completely eliminated. All expenses of underwriting government would be simplified with tax collectors and tax forms as extinct as the dodo bird. Yet, the way of educational, medical and cultural services, these would be much more plentifully available to each and every citizen without any financial stress or duress.

Let us get the broadest picture of how taxation would be handled. Visualize, if you can, our entire nation fitting within the framework, and jurisdiction, of one giant corporation, not unlike, let us say, General Motors. Technically, every citizen is a part owner of the visualized "national" corporation, with its productive potential, by virtue of being a common shareholder. Now here is the thought for you to encompass. Just as General Motors allocates its gross *total* products of let's say 10 billion dollars for production workers, management, overhead, research, plant schooling, pension plans, and expansion, so would the people's corporation allocate its gross *national* product of perhaps 1 trillion dollars to the same general activities, encompassing 190,000,000 people instead of a few hundred thousand workers and executives.

Can't you see that the whole nation becomes one coordinated enterprise, meeting all costs and expenses out of its own productive potential? It would be exit for both the usurer and tax collector. No longer could the citizen be forced to pay tribute to either strategists in politics, finance or the military-industrial complex without getting equity in that which his hard-earned dollars helped construct.

To those who say this approach to solving a nation's ills is socialistic or communistic, we say why don't they make the same charge against the corporate structure of the monopolists? Our only change is that the people, all of the people, shall own and direct the National Corporation and thereby all enjoy the good life.

Webster's Collegiate Dictionary defines *tribute* in part as "a tax paid by a subject vassal to his sovereign or lord." A *vassal*, in turn, is defined as "a subject; dependent; servant, sometimes, a slave. From these definitions the large part of our tax program becomes an instrument of serfdom.

A Corporate Commonwealth would mean our true liberation!

~ 28 ~

Pioneer for Commonwealth Idea!

MOST MEN are in a condition of poverty now. Also, we absolutely know that the trusts, as a result of the centralizing of the control of industrial agencies and material resources, operated in connection with their juggling of credits and money, have made us dependent upon the trusts for employment. This is the industrial slavery that the capitalist interests prefer to chattel slavery. If we were chattel slaves, they would have to care for us in sickness and old age, whereas now they are not concerned with us except for the time that we work for them.

Knowing these facts, will the people continue to remain in such a state of bondage? Certainly not! The trusts have taught us the principle of combination. If it is good and profitable for the trusts, it is good and profitable for the people. It would be better to have one great trust created by all the people for their common benefit than to have our actions controlled by several trusts operated for the individual benefit of a few persons. (page *44 "Banking and Currency and the Money Trust")*

Charles A. Lindbergh, Sr., U. S Congressman from
Minnesota --- 1908-1918

~ 29 ~

"Whatsoever ye do unto the least of these . . . "

WHEN the disciples appeared before Jesus, saying, "Who is the greatest in the kingdom of heaven?" He is reported to have answered, "Verily I say unto you except ye be converted, and become as little children, ye shall not enter the kingdom of heaven." There is so much food for thought in this answer that we wish to give it some consideration. Perhaps we may gain a fresh perspective in so doing.

It is in a child that we observe genuineness of logic and an innate desire for freedom. He wants to be a participant in the game of life, and persistently contends for fulfillment of both his needs and natural urges.

A child is not born with wrong concepts, prejudices and an irreverence for life. He has an inborn capacity to be good, and fair, and constructive if given the opportunity. He is not afraid of being ostracized for asking obvious questions. Nothing is so "sacred" that it cannot be probed into and its worth determined.

ANY normal child knows that if the family basement is lined with shelf upon shelf of canned goods, the family deep-freeze is loaded to the brim, with frozen meats and vegetable, and the refrigerator is filled to capacity, there is no need for him and his brothers and sisters to go hungry. What look of astonishment and suspicion would appear on his face if he were told that there wasn't enough food to nourish their little bodies because there was too much food!

Can't you envision the distrust and misgivings that would be the child's if one morning he was witness to his parents carting out foodstuffs to a storage tank in the backyard which was then locked, or the family truck was loaded with crates of food to be driven away to the opposite end of town? Wouldn't the child exert his right to survive by demanding reasons for storing food, or shipping it "abroad," while all the time his own body was famished?

The story is told of the eight-year-old who within earshot of a number of "learned" economists who were wrestling with the problem of over-production. Listening intently the child was able to brush aside all the professional terms of "marginal profits," "stabilizer factors" and "consumer indexes" and penetrate to the heart of the problem. Realizing that the dilemma was only one of too much wheat, too much corn, too much beef, and too much food of every kind, he eagerly, and with little regard for professional decorum, blurted out for all to hear, "Why don't the people eat it?"

The child knows instinctively that the only purpose for food is to nourish gnawing stomachs. His mind has not yet been conditioned to accept the twisted reasoning that planned scarcity is a virtue and exorbitant profits take precedence over satisfying the needs of human beings.

When we consider the child's whole world of miniature tools, building blocks and assembly kits, we also observe his natural enthusiasm for logical expression. He demands full opportunity of exploring and using their full potential. He can see no logical reason for restricting their employment. His mind unreservedly tells him that "things" should be at his disposal and not that they should circumscribe his functioning.

We could illustrate indefinitely how a child is true to his inherent curiosity, how he has a natural inclination to love life and protect it, and how he seeks uninhibited expression and freedom of movement. There are no limitations to either his yearnings or aspirations.

The world is before him and he wants to explore and conquer all its hidden depths and pathways stretching ever upward.

What an indictment of current civilization that has created a stultified environment within which a child is alienated from himself. It is society that has destroyed his natural love and replaced it with prejudice, suspicion and hatred. It is society that has substituted the unethical conduct for the Golden Rule that advancement might be achieved at the expense of others.

What hypocrisy to call ourselves "Christians" when the precepts of the Man of Peace have been so violated. What audacity to speak of treating our fellowman as we wish him to treat us when our whole society is predicated on the premise of everyone for himself and let the devil take the hindmost.

What unadulterated gall to profess belief in the ministry of the Man of Nazareth who walked the shores of Galilee attending the injured, healing the sick and serving his fellowman, when we show such indifference to the millions hungry, cold and helpless.

THE Man of Peace was not a namby-pamby sentimentalist who spoke in hushed tones lest he be overheard indicting wrongness. He was an actionist, a doer of good deeds, an advocate of social reform that the least amongst men might enjoy the good life. He kowtowed to no one and formed a scourge of cords and drove the moneychangers from the temple.

He practiced what he professed and He said, "By their fruits ye shall know them." He was a seditionist to the abnormal forces of His day and they slew Him for His "tipping over of existing institutions."

Few are the church institutions of today that would even recognize Him if He made an announced appearance. They are too engrossed in holding suppers, catering to their financial supporters and furnishing chaplains for the millions trained to hate and kill.

Not knowing His identity, they would discredit His precepts and His acts of mercy. They would be in the forefront, shouting, "Crucify him, crucify him!"

Yes, there is a poignant lesson to be learned from Jesus when He said, "Whoso shall serve one such little child in my name receiveth me. But whoso shall offend one of these little ones which believe in me, it were better for him that a millstone were hanged about his neck, and that he were drowned in the depth of the sea."

Look at the next little child you see, be he black or white, be he yours or a neighbor's, and get the import of Jesus' message. Then think of the hundreds of millions of children who have been placed in our care, and whose future is in our hands. *Will we be equal to the trust that is ours?*

~ 30 ~

A Look at Ourselves from a Higher Vantage Point

ALL OF US know of the businessman, faced with bankruptcy who removed himself completely from his business and observed, from a broader perspective the bottlenecks causing his failure. From afar he could detect the barriers preventing the release of his productive potential. Actually, his business contained all the necessary ingredients, manpower, know-how and machinery, but they weren't co-coordinated or directed for maximum production. Upon his return, our businessman had only to institute reorganization and his business was successful.

If we could do the same as our businessman in respect to the bottlenecks of this nation's business, we too could detect the errors of our ways. Let us assume that we could persuade NASA to boost us into orbit around the world in a space-rocket. We can identify our mission as "Perspective Humanity." Our purpose would embody nothing more or less than that we are seeking solitude and the opportunity to make a candid and unpressured survey of the nation and the world below us. From a broader perspective we want to take a hard but compassionate look at our society and see what is wrong with it.

Assuming our mission was granted, and we found ourselves far removed from the everyday grind of eking out an existence, the paying of confiscatory taxes, and the restrictive prejudices of traditional thinking, what would be our appraisal of our national business that is now materially and morally on the verge of bankruptcy? Boiled down, the primary conclusion would be simply this: We are a nation that has major *unmet* needs at the same time that it has *unused* productive capacity. Would we not find these two circumstances irreconcilable?

In fact, when we relate these circumstances to children hungry in the midst of food surpluses, to the sick neglected when we could build more than enough hospitals, and to millions uneducated when we could build more than enough schools, shouldn't we clearly recognize the social dereliction of the society we live in? Wouldn't our hearts sicken at hardships endured when the potential exists to erase all such hardships?

So our first observation from the higher vantage point would be this: Our nation is not lacking in a single ingredient, man-power, tools or the know-how, by which to meet to surfeit all the needs of the entire citizenry. This nation has a perfected technology of the moment, which can produce everything for a secure and prosperous life for each and every citizen. There need not be 30,000,000 of our citizens living in poverty. There need not be one-third of our families living in unsound, dilapidated houses. There need not be insufficient hospitals to care for the ill or any lack of schools to educate our children. And there need not be millions of meaningless roles in society leading to breakdown and violence.

With this premise, we in our hypothetical spaceship would automatically direct our attention to the obvious question: Why can't our nation, and its citizenry, employ its unused capacity to do those things that need to be done in order to provide the wholesome and meaningful life for every individual? In whose interest and at whose behest is our nation governed so that want abounds amidst plenty? What is wrong with our economic and political structure that large segments of society can be excluded from having even material necessities or a chance to improve themselves?

Looking down on our national household, so preoccupied with acceleration that it doesn't see its lack of direction, some startling observations are forced upon us. Foremost is the conclusion that the whole premise upon which the nation's business is conducted has been wrong from the beginning, although only recently have technological developments made its inequities so apparent. We have been blinded to the reality that our whole economic and social structure is premised on nothing but the Law of the Jungle.

Instead of the whole approach to meeting the needs of the people being based on working together that the minimum effort might be expended to provide the good life, each individual is instead sent out into the "market place" to fend for himself and let the devil take the hindmost.

It is a system of economic savagery with a premium on beating the next fellow. If you buy a horse for fifty dollars, you are morally justified under our present system in charging your neighbor one hundred dollars for it, despite the fact that you had neither curried it nor fed it during your temporary ownership. If a corporation can produce an item for twenty-five dollars, counting all expenses, it is justified in charging thirty-five dollars for each item simply on the basis that its seductive advertising inveigled its customers to pay that much.

All the exhortations in the name of "free competition," and the "free market," cannot alter the inescapable fact that the gimmick of *profit* is false and evil when it represents earnings for which no human effort was expended. As such it must, and should, be identified as sheer thievery.

Of course, when one is enmeshed in the prevailing struggle, it sounds quite plausible to be told that profit is earnings on investment, or is inducement to work or to start an enterprise, but when the siphoning-off process is viewed candidly and without personal involment, the ruthlessness of its function is deadly evident. It becomes crystal clear that while one transaction of a fifty-dollar horse sold for a hundred dollars may not seriously disrupt the economy, it is this fraud multiplied literally millions of times each day that has concentrated the wealth and power of our whole economy into the hands of only a few to the detriment of the many.

No more insidious propaganda exists than that advanced by the power-structures that for a nation to coordinate its productive potential for use, not profit and power, is somehow "communistic or socialistic." And just because some fellow by the name of Marx also made some similar reference to "use" as the end result of production, millions of good Americans parrot the power structures' ideology that any alternative to the debt-profit economy is based on a foreign "ism." The real irony lies in the fact that the power structures of private banking, monopolistic industry and political machines are doing exactly what they are telling their victims they can't and shouldn't do. They have planned, organized and coordinated the whole economy for their *private use and power.* Why is it, then, an unpardonable sin for the whole people, reflecting the true wealth and credit of the nation, to restore economic sovereignty to themselves by planning, organizing and coordinating the whole economy for the benefit of each and every citizen?

From a distant spaceship, a most intriguing observation could be made. Like a break in the weather, or a light suddenly turned on, it dawns on us that if the corporate structure has worked so successfully as a coordinated business for the few, what is to prevent the adoption of the same framework for operating a successful national business for all? What a stroke of fate if the very instrument that has disadvantaged and disserviced so many people can be employed constructively truly to serve them all!

It is not difficult to establish the fact that since the inception of this nation it has been the *unearned* profits, represented by usury, price-fixing, money-manipulation, rents and liens of all forms, that have ultimately lodged the natural resources and productive assets in the iron grip of a mere handful of corporations. The entire *modus operandi* of capitalism has been a process of systematically excluding larger and larger segments from the economy in both the areas of ownership and purchasing power. Of this moment, it is the taxpayers' dollars underwriting the monopolies' billions of dollars in research and the consumers' dollars paid in fixed prices that are accelerating the final takeover.

From the beginning this nation should have had *public* capitalism instead of *private* capitalism. This would have meant that the people would have automatically been stockholders, both dividend-receiving and voting in all corporations commensurate with their inherent claim upon all natural resources and their individually earned claims as contributors and consumers. Belatedly, this is what must come to pass. There is no other realistic solution to providing genuine purchasing power to the people in order that they can buy what a technological economy can produce. All else is charity and tyranny of government through the bureaucratic administration of welfarism.

A CORPORATE COMMONWEALTH, or a nationally incorporated economy, can best be envisioned by taking any one of the multi-billion-dollar corporations and expanding it to take in the entire nation. More and more the larger corporations are expanding to include many diversified products, so the functioning of one nationwide, coordinated enterprise producing all goods and services would be only bigger in scope of operations. Clear in our thinking should be the realization that ownership and decision-making should be held democratically in the hands of all the people, including every worker, manager, researcher, serviceman and other person engaged in making products or performing all services. There would be no similarity to any of the forms of state ownership to which there is much justified objection. The profit motive, with all its attendant inequities, would be eliminated and all purchasing power would be distributed solely on the basis of equity in, and contribution to, the Commonwealth.

The innovation of a Corporate Commonwealth would mark the end of all built-in obsolescence. The biggest renovation would be the end of any reliance on the private banker, with his whole gamut of interest, debt and mortgages against future earnings. Checking accounts established with each citizen would be secured by the total production of both goods and services which have been produced by the whole people who will in turn consume and use them. The only limitation on what could be enjoyed would be the limitation of the nation's maximum productive capability.

For the first time every person could be a meaningful participant in society. His guaranteed income would remove any threat of not providing food, shelter and clothing for himself and his family. Efficiency in work would be translated into more time to travel, devote efforts in creative pursuits or further one's education.

From a higher vantage point, the corporate structure is no different than the unlimited power of nuclear energy. It, too, can be employed either for the destruction of man or for his inestimable benefit.

Are we now ready to use both for peace and the wholesome life for all mankind?

On War Psychoses
Mark Twain

"I can see a million years ahead, and this rule will never change in as many as half a dozen instances. The loud little handful as usual, will shout for war. The pulpit will wearily and cautiously object, at first.

The great big mass of the nation will rub its sleepy eyes and try to make out why there should be a war, and will say, earnestly and indignantly, 'It's unjust and dishonorable and there is no necessity for it.'

Then the handful will shout louder. A few fair men on the other side will argue and reason against the war with speech and pen, and at first will have a hearing and be applauded.

Before long, you will see this curious thing: The speakers stoned from their platform and free speech strangled by hordes of furious men who in their secret hearts are still at one with the stoned speakers, as earlier, but do not dare to say so now.

And the whole nation, pulpit and all, will take up the war cry and shout itself hoarse, and mob any honest man who ventures to open his mouth, and presently such mouths will cease to open.

Next the statesmen will invent cheap lies, putting the blame on that nation that attacked, and every man will be glad of those conscience-soothing falsities and will diligently study them.

And thus he will, by and by, convince himself that the war is just, and will thank God for the better sleep he enjoys after this process of grotesque self-deception."

~ 31 ~

Impeachment ---
Secrecy in government
Our Monetary Mess

(Periodically, Rep. Wright Patman puts out releases to his mailing list, not at government expense. We believe the facts and conclusions of the latest, October 24, 1966 deserves widest possible circulation.)

IS Impeachment Necessary?

How else can we get a full and public review of the closed-door operations of the Federal Reserve Board?

All other agencies of the Federal Government come before Congress annually for authorizations and appropriations. At the same time, the activities of the agencies are reviewed in great detail. Through the years, this has prevented the bureaucrats from losing sight of the public interest. As a further safeguard, these same agencies are subject to audit by the General Accounting Office.

But, the Federal Reserve Board does not come to Congress for appropriations. Its books are not audited by the General Accounting Office. As a result, the Congress, the President, and the American people are completely in the dark about what is going on at the Federal Reserve.

With monetary conditions worsening, many are wondering just how the Congress and the American people can get behind this heavy veil of secrecy. While the power has seldom been used, it remains a fact that impeachment proceedings can force an agency and its officials to lay bare behind-the-scenes operations.

Such a move is drastic and serious. It should be used with great care and considered only when the public interest has been grossly violated.

But this country, as a result of high interest rates, is facing a serious problem and major disruptions in its economy. It may well take drastic remedies to correct a drastically bad situation.

Under the present situation, it is not suprising that the Federal Reserve Board would thumb its nose at the President, the Congress and the people. This situation is ready-made for such defiance.

CIA-like Secrecy

Outside of the top secret Central Intelligence Agency, no agency in our Federal Government operates with more secrecy than the Federal Reserve. As Chairman of the House Banking and Currency Committee, I have consistently attempted to get information on the manipulations of the Federal Reserve's Open Market Committee.

The Federal Reserve Open Market Committee meets every three weeks to determine interest rates and the supply of money available in the economy. Through its power to contract and expand the money supply, it has almost life or death control of the economy. The meetings are held behind locked doors at the Federal

Reserve and no member of the Congress or the Executive Branch is allowed inside.

In fact, the only information that the Banking and Currency committee has been able to obtain is for meetings conducted in 1960 or earlier. We cannot get anything more recent. In other words, the Federal Reserve will not release information on these top-secret meetings until the statue of limitations has run. So if there were any illegal acts, we would not find out about them until it was too late to prosecute.

The Open Market Committee, of course, operates as a private affair and the public is left out of all deliberations. Yet, this body is a prime factor in an economy in which all the people have a direct stake.

By law, the Open Market Committee is limited to the seven members of the Federal Reserve Board and five of the twelve presidents of the Federal Reserve banks. In practice, however, all twelve presidents of the Federal Banks have participated in the meetings. The bank presidents in turn represent the commercial banking interests in their districts. For example, out of the total of 108 directors in the twelve Federal Reserve Banks, 84 are or have been connected with the private banking industry. So it is plain---the Open Market Committee is an "insider's club" for the bankers.

The banks know about the secret decisions of the Open Market Committee within minutes after their meeting is closed. At least 2,000 top bankers are able to get hold of this inside information almost immediately. The opportunities for the banks to profit from this information are limitless. Yet, the public's elected representatives are kept in the dark about these meetings.

Such "inside dealings," limited to an elite few, have always characterized policy making in totalitarian states. Such an arrangement for policy making has no place in a free and democratic society.

Should the American People Pay Twice?

The secrecy situation is but one example of the Federal Reserve's strange method of operation. Certainly, one of the most fantastic examples of the Federal Reserve's "Public-Be-Damned" attitude is illustrated in its portfolio of $42 billion worth of U. S. bonds. These are bonds which have been paid for once; yet, the Federal Reserve continues to hold these bonds and to charge the taxpayers $1.7 billion in interest annually.

This is comparable to a citizen paying off a loan on his automobile and continuing to send the bank a check for interest every month. No one, of course, would voluntarily enter into such a nonsensical arrangement. Yet, the United States taxpayers are caught in just such a situation when the Treasury annually pays out the $1.7 billion in interest on the $42 billion worth of bonds held by the Federal Reserve Bank of New York.

The Federal Reserve uses these interest payments to carry on its far-flung operations. It pays the salaries, the huge expense accounts, and other incidentals of the Board with this fund. Included are about $90 thousand in annual dues to the American Bankers Association and various state and local banking associations, which in turn, lobby for the bank interests. Since there is no audit, no one really knows what happens to all of this money in any given year.

More important, the $1.7 billion fund, created by the interest charges on the $42 billion worth of bonds, enables the Federal Reserve Board to operate *without coming to Congress for appropriations.* Of course, if the Federal Reserve did come to Congress for appropriations, it would have to reveal its secrets and its innermost manipulations of the American economy.

Current Effects of Federal Reserve Policy

No longer are we engaged in academic discussions when we talk about the Federal Reserve's secrecy, the $42 billion worth of bonds its dodging of the appropriations and auditing processes. The end result has been the evolution of an agency, which takes care of the banks first, and the public last. With the public and the public's representatives completely shut out, the Federal Reserve has moved more and more into the banker's hands.

This is why the Federal Reserve moved so rapidly last December fifth to take care of the big banks' needs for higher interest rates. The big banks, primarily those located in Chicago and New York, asked the Federal Reserve to raise interest rates by *37-1/2 %* so that they could hold onto a large block of time deposits (certificates of deposit). The Federal Reserve, acting with almost automatic response, immediately granted the request.

To make the move look plausible, the Federal Reserve immediately issued propaganda releases claiming that they were acting to prevent inflation. What they did, of course, was to add to the cost of every item in the economy through higher interest rates and thereby feed the fires of inflation. The Federal Reserve's claims about inflation are simply an excuse and a smokescreen to hide a blatant, special benefit to a handful of big banks which faced the loss of large time deposits.

In order to do this, the Federal Reserve was willing to defy the President of the United States, the Congress and the American people. They could do this because they knew they did not have to come to Congress for appropriations. They knew they could not be penalized in any meaningful fashion.

What the Defense Has Cost

While the banks have profited in the past year, the people have been hurt severely by high interest rates.

The interest on the public debt has gone up about $1 billion annually just as a result of this single action of the Federal Reserve Board. This is money out of the pockets of every taxpayer.

Right now, when the Treasury borrows $1 million, it must pay $50 thousand in interest in just one year. During World War II, the Treasury could borrow this same $1 million and pay only $3,750 in interest. In other words, the cost of Government borrowing has gone up more than *13* times since World War II.

The cost of financing state governments, local governments, and school districts has also risen sharply. In many cases, school districts are being forced to stop building classrooms because interest rates are too high. In other cases, the high cost of interest is draining off funds from other needed educational projects. Cities and counties are foregoing plans for water and sewage facilities.

The housing industry has been particularly hard hit, and today it is becoming very difficult for many Americans to obtain decent housing because of high interest rates. Residential housing will drop almost 20% in 1966 and the trend will continue into the next year.

Remember, a $20,000 home today will require more than $23,168 in interest over the life of a 30-year mortgage. A 1% increase in interest on a $20,000 house represents almost $4,800 in additional interest charges. That means that many Americans have to work a full year just to pay this additional interest charge.

If high interest rates continue, we are almost certain to see the country slip into a recession or a depression.

What Can Be Done?

Recently, a newspaper columnist wrote about the Federal Reserve System and said:

"It all seems rather strange in a free and open society."

Yes, it is strange and it is even stranger that the Congress has not met its responsibility in the area of monetary affairs. The 90th Congress, which will convene in January, should make reform of monetary policy a priority legislative item.

Somehow, the Federal Reserve must be brought to account for its dereliction of duty and for its gross manipulation of the economy in favor of the banks.

In the 90th Congress, I will introduce legislation to bring the Federal Reserve System back under the control of the people and their elected representatives. My bill will require that the terms of the members of the Federal Reserve be reduced from fourteen years to five years and that the term of the chairman be made coterminous with that of the President of the United States. The Bill will also direct that the Federal Reserve come to the Congress for annual appropriations and that most of the $42 billion in bonds, presently held by the Federal Reserve, be retired. The Bill would direct the Federal

235

Reserve to open its books to General Accounting Office audit and to make public the records of the Open Market Committee.

Earlier in this newsletter, I mention the word "impeachment". Impeachment is a seldom used but effecttive instrument to achieve necessary objectives when a recalcitrant individual is improperly blocking the progress of the nation. A case in point is Andrew W. Mellon, who was made Secretary of the Treasury in 1921. Immediately after his appointment to office, Secretary Mellon assumed policies that would benefit the great rich, to the detriment of the poor. He commenced immediately, without authority of law, to have all activities of the twelve Federal Reserve banks centralized under control of the New York Federal Reserve Bank. This has been the way the system has operated ever since that time. (And this is the principal cause of the high interest tight money policy that is so ruinous to day!)

In addition, he bitterly opposed payment of the adjusted compensation to the veterans of World War I which amounted to an average of $1,015 for each of 3-1/2 million veterans. Realizing the full implications of Secretary Mellon's roadblock tactics, I filed impeachment proceedings against him. After three weeks of hearings before the House Judiciary Committee, and within the hour before he was scheduled to testify, he submitted his resignation to President Hoover, who then announced Mellon's appointment as Ambassador to the Court of St. James. In effect, this was a Presidential pardon in the middle of a trial. Soon thereafter, the veterans got their money through legislation, which I sponsored.

When all else fails, the impeachment process is a remedy to be kept in mind; possibly its use should be considered now.

Whatever is done will depend largely on the people of the United States. If you want action, you must let your elected representatives at all levels---the House of Representatives, the United States Senate, and the President---know your desires. The 90th Congress will act if the demand from the people grows strong enough.

With elections only a short time away, you have the best opportunity to look over the candidates and to urge them to support policies that will bring about lower interest rates and a sound monetary system. We can never have a sound monetary system until that system is designed to be responsible to the people and the people's elected representatives.

I pledge to make a real fight in the 90th Congress for reform of the Federal Reserve and for lower interest rates. But the real decision rests in your hands. What will you do about this before the 90th Congress convenes in January?

Representative Wright Patman

~ 32 ~

The Problem Is Still With Us!

"ALL THE PERPLEXITIES, CONFUSION AND DISTRESS IN AMERICA ARISE, NOT FROM DEFECTS IN THEIR CONSTITUTION OR CONFEDERATION, NOT FROM WANT OF HONOR OR VIRTUE, SO MUCH AS FROM DOWNRIGHT IGNORANCE OF THE NATURE OF COIN, CREDIT AND CIRCULATION."

John Adams in a letter to Thomas Jefferson

~ 33 ~

Cooperative Co-existence, Not War, Is the Imperative Of our Times

By Hugh B. Hester

Peace has no more ardent advocate than Hugh B. Hester, Brigadier General, U. S. Army (Ret.). Having served in the U. S. Army for over thirty years, he participated in both World Wars and was decorated for gallantry in action by the French and U. S. Governments in WWI. He was also awarded the United States Distinguished Service Medal and the French Legion of Honor for service in WWII.

IF PRESIDENT JOHNSON will stop his illegal, immoral and genocidal war against the Vietnamese people, a war which is degrading every American, he will have no need to urge, as recently, the State Governors or any others, to curb an inflation which falls heaviest upon the poorest, while providing vast profits for a few. But war's unequal burdens and inequities do not end with inflation and the inability of the poor to procure the necessities, such as clothing, food and shelter. It also extends to battle casualties.

If the records of killed and wounded in Vietnam were published, they would, I am confident, reveal that the vast majority of casualties came from those families who have less than average educational and cultural advantages, and opportunities. Selective service regulations are set up that way. General Hershey, Director of Selective Service, has publicly stated that there were enough student dropouts and non-students to supply the major military re-quirements. The McNamara training program for these not meeting military standards point in the same direction. The cannon fodder in the electronic-nuclear age, as in all other ages, apparently will continue to be supplied in the main by the least privileged, those with nothing to win.

At no previous time in history could the statement attributed to General N. Bradley, during the Korean War that "we are fighting the wrong war, against the wrong enemy, at the wrong place and the wrong time," be more aptly applied than to the present Vietnamese War. The greatest enemy of the people is poverty

This enemy is clearly visible in our slums, in our race relations, and in the increase of violence and other de-linquencies by both adults and juveniles. The very con-servative and usually calm Mr. Lippman, just before leaving for Europe, put it this way in the August 1st, 1966, issue of *Newsweek*: "The condition of our cities, where the majority of our people live, is explosive, not only because of the black ghettos, but also because these cities are becoming progressively unlivable for everyone, black or white. These cities demand our paramount attention. They need great sums of money. Neither attention nor money is available now that the Administration has gone off whoring after false gods in pursuit of World Power."

This grab for "world power," we must however in fairness state, did not originate with the Johnson Administration. It began with the Truman Administration and has been followed by every Washington Administration since. It began immediately after President Roosevelt's death.

Professor Fleming, in his encyclopedic two-volume history of "The Cold War and its Origins," describes in detail how Mr. Truman and his colleagues dragged the cold war out from under the World War II rug where it had been buried for the duration, and began the vast propaganda brain-washing program which has continued in intensified form ever since.

This abrupt and basic change in U. S. government foreign policy by the Truman Administration has had far-reaching and disastrous results. It has dangerously divided the world. The pursuit of this policy has resulted in the division of Germany and the rearmament of the Bonn portion of Germany in violation of every professed purpose for waging war against Hitler. And this rearmament of Germany (Hitler's Nazi remnant), as the distinguished former foreign service officer, Mr. George F. Kennan, pointed out in *Look* magazine, November 19th 1963, has made genuine friendly relations with the Soviet Union very difficult, if not impossible.

The continued pursuit of this tragic shift, initiated by the Truman Administration, has also forced China out of her Charter Seat in the United Nations. And in turn, this has destroyed the potential capacity of that world organization to make peace in Asia, or even to bid on making it there.

In summary, this tragically wrong turn in foreign policy making at the end of World War II has made World War III all but inevitable. President Johnson still has the power, even late as it is, I believe, to prevent such a disaster. But to do this, he will have to abandon completely the Truman dream of world domination and rule. He will have to devote all the power of his great office and the resources of this great country to conquering poverty, the most dangerous enemy of man everywhere.

As a beginning and immediate program, the President could and should stop the war in Southeast Asia and end U. S. diplomatic, economic and political warfare in Red China. He should start the liquidation of U. S. Special Military Forces, now located throughout the Asian, African and Latin American countries, and begin to bring home the large bodies of U. S. military forces located in Europe, Asia and the Western Pacific. All of these are necessary, I believe, to reduce present world tension to manageable proportions. And these can be accomplished by the President with the minimum of opposition from outside, or need for consultation with other countries and the Congress.

As a follow-up to the reduction in tensions resulting from the above acts, the President should start serious negotiations for ending the arms race, now consuming almost all resources that could and should be made available for a worldwide war on poverty. He should start the development of a program, in consultation with the other countries, for the proper use of excess funds of all countries saved through the reduction in the arms race. And this program should provide first, for ending poverty at home, second, for ending poverty elsewhere and finally that all aid funds, whatever the source, for third parties be coordinated through the United Nations and administered through UN Agency, perhaps patterned after the old United Nations Relief and Rehabilitation Agency (UNRRA).

Simultaneously with the above, I believe, the President should promote the following things in the international field: First, he should urge the universalization of membership in the United Nations, regardless of economic, political and social philosophies, or the claim by any nation that such and such nation is not "peace loving." Second, he should promote the maximization of trade without discrimination such as "the favored nation clause," or other clauses. Third, he should promote the freedom of all people to travel regardless of their economic, political and social concepts. Fourth, he should promote the maximum exchange among countries of all cultural activities and scientific and other information. Fifth and finally, the President should promote and urge the discovery of an independent source of revenue to adequately finance the necessary activities of the United Nations.

If the President will seriously attempt to accomplish the things enumerated above, even though he should fail on some, I am convinced he will render great service to mankind and be recognized as a leading benefactor of man; perhaps even the greatest benefactor. On the other hand, if he continues to follow the grab for world domination, initiated by M. Truman and followed more or less by General Eisenhower and Mr. Kennedy, to its logical conclusion, as currently, he will probably go down in history (if there is one) as man's greatest malefactor.

~ 34 ~

LOVE OF HUMANITY

Civilization must be judged and prized, not by the amount of power it has developed, but by how much it has evolved and given expression to, by its laws and institutions, the love of humanity.

--- Sadhana, 1914

(Rabindranath Tagore on Civilization and Humanity)

~ 35 ~

True Force for Peace ---
the People!

On THE morning of May 11th, Secretary of Defense
appeared before the Senate Foreign Relations Committee. Three hours later, at the conclusion of his
testimony, it was made known that there would be no
further public hearings on Vietnam. All sessions thereafter would be held behind closed doors.

Whether all future hearings will be "executive" sessions
or whether a supposedly sovereign people will be given
spasmodic glimpses into the functioning of government
is begging the issue. At this point serious conclusions
can be drawn. It is hoped that the larger segment of
the television viewers got the full import of what
transpired.

Fully appreciating that much enlightenment has e-
merged from the hearings, and a small minority of the
members did evince statesmanship qualities, an over-
all assessment of "government" in action compels a
serious indictment. And that indictment is this:
*Representative government, as an informed expression
of the people's wishes and best interests, in non-existent.*

Aquila followed each televised hearing most intently
with the optimism that there would develop a Committee consensus which would recognize the pur-

poseless and needless killing underlying the whole Vietnam War. We speculated, perhaps too prayerfully, that somehow the mounting evidence, accentuating our own untenable position, coupled with the inherent dangers of escalated war, would convince the most callous members as to the immorality and brutality of our continued involvement.

It is now evident that our optimism was projected more on our heartfelt desires than on the realism of current political structure.

The realism of current political structure! This is the key to an understanding of why the serious challenges to the nation's well-being and safety, both at home and abroad, are not honestly confronted. In bluntest terms it must be faced that the vast majority who make up the Congress of the nation are there at the behest of the power structures entrenched in our midst and not in the capacity, or with the motivation, to serve the people. It is against this backdrop that solutions to all major issues must be considered.

Any other approach is both puerile and unrealistic.

The hearings before the Senate Foreign Relations Committee, because some were televised, should have been a real object lesson to many Americans on just how inefficiently and undemocratically "representative" government operates. Certainly there is no elected Committee in the entire Congress that should be more scrutinized and evaluated. On its shoulders rests the chief responsibility to pass on the question of war or peace. In their hands rests the question of life or death of every able-bodied man and boy in this nation who has or will be drafted into the armed services.

Dereliction of Responsibility

The first thing that must have registered with most viewers was the fact that at all hearings many of the members were not even present. One would have thought, if for no other reason, the majority of members would have been present simply to put on a good political "front." While a few could have had valid commitments, it is unpardonable that consistently the majority of seats were vacant when men occupying the highest offices of the War Administration were being questioned.

Such wanton absence, irrespective of position regarding Vietnam, is not only dereliction of responsibility but underscores the whole myth of checks and balances, and precludes the paramount right of every citizen to pass judgment on his representatives while they are discharging their offices.

Perhaps Senator Thomas Dodd of Connecticut, in one of his painful and passing presences at the hearings, expressed the inner feelings of his fellow absentees when he brazenly exclaimed that at best the hearings were a "drag" on conducting the nation's business that must perhaps be tolerated within the scope of the democratic framework. Never was a more contemptible statement uttered.

We contend, unequivocally, that no man is qualified to hold public office, even the lowliest of offices, whose view is that the sovereignty of the people is simply something to be tolerated. Such irresponsible utterance is clear evidence of an officeholder's loyalty belonging to someone other than the electorate.

No discerning person could have witnessed the hearings without concluding that only about one-quarter of the 19-member Committee displayed any real competence or objectivity. Outside of Chairman Fullbright, Senator Morse and a very few others, the balance of the Committee, when they were present, showed that they had neither a historical grasp of Southeast Asia, particularly Vietnam, nor any basic comprehension of the right of any people to work out their own destinies without outside interference.

Only the ten-minute limitation on questioning saved the majority from being completely stripped of the thin veneer of respectability with which they have been politically enshrouded.

A Sovereign People

At this point we want to stress, as we have constantly stressed in this publication, that ultimately it must come to pass that a people to be truly sovereign must make the final judgment on all major policy and legislation. This is doubly true in the case of war when prejudiced and incompetent decisions mean the needless loss of lives and endanger the very survival of all mankind.

Despite all the confusion and false exhortations in the name of freedom that characterized the hearings, it is the belief of Aquila that if the television viewers could pass on the Vietnam War the majority would vote for this nation's withdrawal. While there are many basic reasons contended by dispassionate scholars, particularly in the field of international law as to why we should withdraw, it is our belief that the majority of viewers would call a halt to our participation on three broad considerations. They would be as follows:

1. There is no validity to our commitment. From the beginning we have supported nothing but military juntas which have never represented the rank and file of the Vietnamese people. The present Ky Regime is unstable, corrupt and despotic. *There is justification for civil war,* and *rebellion against the colonial-oriented, puppet regime in Saigon.*

2. We are engaged in an open-ended war with no goals that lead to peace through realistic negotiations. This can only mean increased loss of American lives, inevitable clash with China and possibly Russia, and the unleashing of World War III. Nuclear war with the literal annihilation of hundreds of millions of human beings is unthinkable. *Such reckless coarse is devoid of sanity and cannot be equated with peace or security.*

3. The American heart has become sickened by the brutality of war. It has become increasingly difficult to morally justify the mightiest nation in the world destroying the land and killing the inhabitants of a weak and much smaller nation in the name of humaneness or establishing the right of self-determination. *Something in the spiritual make-up of man rebels spontaneously against such overdrawn circumstance.*

The only militating factor against the foregoing would be the promoted obsession that China is out to conquer the world. However, many Americans are commencing to see the illogic of charging China with aggression when we have encircled her with nuclear bases, and have summarily excluded her from having any voice in world councils.

Political Tyranny

If our assessment of the broad feelings of the Americans is correct, is it not apparent that the Senate Foreign Relations Committee, acting in behalf of the Senate, have thwarted the sovereign will of the people by failing to check the war administration in its undeclared war? In short, if the people exercised their supreme power there would be no Americans dying ten thousand miles from our own shores.

As harsh as the indictment may seem to some people we as a nation have become the unsuspecting victim of political tyranny within our own borders. It did not happen overnight. Over the years the economic and banking power structures have succeeded in building parallel political machines which have screened only those who would do the bidding of their financial masters.

Most of those so elected have felt no real obligation either to pursue peace or to put our economic house in order. Both such achievements are anathema to political, industrial and military oligarchies which have fattened on economic spoils both here and around the globe.

Special credit is due those men in Congress who, despite their small numbers, have rebelled against the designs of power structures. While they may momentarily be compelled to suffer penalties, they will go down in history as men whom the spoils of office could not buy.

Senator Morse has posed the issue confronting the nation as one between "bullets and ballots." If the electorate in this fall election is unable to elect 40 to 50 new members to Congress who are opposed to the Vietnam escalation, he foresees little chance of preventing World War III.

Never were there times so fraught with life-and-death challenges. Failure of the people to act can only spell disaster for all mankind.

New Brand of Patriotism

Across the breath and length of this land Americans must challenge all forms of prostituted power. Openly and valorously they must take their stands against all war, all poverty, all ignorance and all prejudices. While a nation, or a world, cannot be renovated in weeks, or months, the only barrier to a solving of all problems is the people's own timidity in exercising their absolute sovereignty.

A new brand of patriotism is required. It must be more than emotional love of country. It must encompass a reverence for all life irrespective of race or nationality. Above all it must be a realistic patriotism that moves the people to order their own human relationships so that compassion for each other can become a living reality.

Under a Corporate Commonwealth both political sovereignty, as well aa economic sovereignty, would be assured for all the people. Every solitary human being would be a voting participant in society and would have an inviolate equity in the ability of the nation to produce everything to abundance.

In that day there could be no spoils of office to subvert the minds and hearts of men. *It would be the true basis for peace and Brotherhood.*

251

~ 36 ~

Before Conquering Space, Let's Learn How to Live on Earth

By Jerry Voorhis
President of the Cooperative League

(Reprinted from *The Cooperative Consumer,*
February28, 1966)

THERE is so much hardware orbiting the earth that traffic lanes for satellites may soon be necessary.

"Moon shots" are becoming almost commonplace.

Writers and speakers confidently predict that computers will soon replace countless presently employed people.

Communication around the globe is instantaneous. And before long, transportation will be almost so.

No longer is it "science fiction" to speak of how the pressing of a few buttons could release enough destructive missiles to devastate whole nations. This is just plain science.

It is science of one particular sort---physical or military science.

But there is another kind of science which has been neglected. It is social science---the science that could teach us how to live together. It's a science that some cooperatives have learned quite well.

Some basic principles of the science of living together were laid down long ago.

"Thou shalt not kill."

"Thou shall love thy neighbor as thyself."

"Inasmuch as you have done it unto one of the least of these my brothers, you have done it unto me."

Dinosaurs were physically mighty. Why they disappeared from the earth is not fully known, but one widely accepted view among scientists is that they disappeared because they were unable to adjust to their changing environment.

Man, too, has become mighty. He has for the first time acquired the power to destroy all or most of the life on earth. Will he be able to adjust to this new situation and remain alive or is he going to follow the footsteps of the dino-saurs?

The next 20 years probably will tell.

For even if we reach the moon, and even if we explore all space, and even if we find out how to create life---none of this will avail us anything if we do not learn to live together in peace and how to win the war on poverty and the war on ignorance and the war on prejudice and the war on pride and arrogance.

Our first task and duty is to develop an order on the earth which is good enough and decent enough reasonably to assure the right of our grandchildren to live at all.

It would be a pity if physical science produced some pieces of squirming protoplasm only to find that our political and social science were unable to prevent mankind from committing suicide in World War III. The protoplasm would be so very lonely!

We Pray the Dolphins Weren't Listening!

A NEWS ITEM the other night has hit us with sickening impact. It has to do with the discovery that Dolphins can differentiate between certain kinds of metals. It follows then that dolphins carrying packs of explosives can be used to destroy enemy submarines, since they could be trained to avoid specially treated American subs. "Of course," the newscaster said, "it would mean the end of the dolphin, but it might save many lives."

What kind of a mind thought that one up? It isn't enough that human beings spend their energy, their time, their money and their blood trying to think ways of destroying each other---they must betray the happiest and friendliest of God's creatures into the same kind of suicidal insanity!

~ 37 ~

People Are Real Arbiters
Of All Reform!

A RECENT visitor to Aquila exclaimed, "If the American people, just a bare majority, could realistically envision the personal freedom and abundant prosperity that would be theirs under a Corporate Commonwealth, they would constitute a real force for social change that could not be deterred." Our visitor had, of course, put into capsule form the national dilemma of the Twentieth Century. Stated in another way, he was simply recognizing that the only barrier to the people's material and spiritual liberation is their own ignorance of what *should* and *can* be done.

One can always make deprecating remarks about the people and their seeming indifference to their own well-being and survival. History is replete with instance after instance where those who have championed the rights of the people have been crucified by the very people whom they were trying to help. However the real tragedy is not the leader's imprisonment or execution but the continued oppression of a people who possess the collective power to eliminate their oppressors summarily.

From the beginning, the founders of Aquila have been under no illusion that they were divinely ordained to save mankind. They know that there is no man, nor group of men, that possess either the wisdom or the rightful power to be so commissioned. They know that the folly of the past has been that the people have sought surcease from their burdens by appealing to the very ones who profit most by the perpetuation of those burdens.

All of Aquila's efforts are premised on the absolute and constant power of the people themselves to effect every and all change that would provide a better and safer life for themselves and their children. The basic role of Aquila is simply to inform and educate the widest number of people that they can effect their own deliverance---permanently eradicating all injustice and needless hardship.

While Aquila was first setup to emphasize and promote the idea, or program, of a *Corporate Commonwealth* as the ultimate goal that must be sought, it became apparent immediately that the people first had to be deconditioned as to the kind of America they thought they lived in, and even more seriously, they must be given analytical understanding of how they are disserviced and disadvantaged by the present economic-financial-political system itself.

At Aquila we are not interested in either palliatives or half-measures. These only deal with the victims of the society and eliminate none of the circumstances that caused the victims in the first place. The times call for leadership to stand forth and make unequivocally clear what is wrong in the nation and what must be done to set it on a course whose guidelines are the inherent rights of each and every human being.

Broadly speaking, the message that must be gotten across to all the people---especially the most destitute and disadvantaged---is that the New Order in human relationships that must be ushered in has to rest four-square on the people's right to be sovereign in working out their economic needs as well as their political needs. Embedded in the people's consciousness must be the irrevocable conviction that they cannot be politically free as long as they have no direct voice in determining their economic freedom.

The time has come when the lowliest, and poorest, in our society must realize that as human beings they have an inherent right to be heard, to participate in that society. They must recognize that they are political slaves when they possess the means to break their shackles but fear to exercise their sovereignty. Such fear can only be removed by a clear understanding, and acceptance, of certain basic premises underscoring all human life and human relationships. The three most important would be as follows:

1. Every human being---irrespective of race, nationality, or possessions or position of parents---is born with the same rights as any other human being. No person is born with fewer rights. No person is born with more rights.

2. Human beings are of paramount importance. Resources, tools, technology, and all forms of social structure---including government itself---have no importance in and of themselves. It is only as these serve and enhance human beings that they have worth and purpose. Man was not meant to serve things. All things were meant to serve man.

3. Supreme power rests in the hands of the people in determining their existence and shaping their future. There is no restraint, injustice or needless hardship

258

that cannot be removed by the people themselves. Neither laws, nor institutions, nor government are above change when such change makes for a better society and the enhancement of human beings.

These premises are not philosophical abstractions. They are just and logical yardsticks by which to measure man's maximum capability for freedom in both expression and movement. It is when we apply these yardsticks to the economic and political history of this nation that we can identify the injustices and "crimes' against humanity in the past, and more importantly, we can determine the basic social reform that must be brought about.

It is only when the poor, the disadvantaged, and the exploited people themselves gain the first realization that they as human beings are as important as any other human beings---that both God and Nature are impartial---that they are inspired with a real desire to be free. How can tens of millions move to liberate themselves when they labor under the promoted misapprehension that they have the same opportunity as others but just haven't measured up in the "competitive open market"?

Unfortunately, despite all the glorious concepts of freedom and opportunity extolled as fundamental to our economic system, capitalism has progressively destroyed both. The common people must come to see that they have been the victims of a system that encourages the most deceitful and most cunning to exploit the majority through the hundred and one guises of the fallacious concepts of *profit*.

The ordinary people must recognize that there can be no moral, or ethical, justification for the whole practice of extracting a price, which exceeds anything contributed to a product or service. Such practice is sheer thievery and should be recognized for what it is. When it has meant the garnering of the nation's assets and resources into the hands of the few, with the majority excluded from living decently and with dignity, then the whole economic system must be brought to an accounting.

However, in bringing private exploitive capitalism to an accounting the people should not make the mistake of accepting the other extreme of State despotism, as under systems of communism or socialism. While you may change the ownership and control of production, you have not eliminated concentration of power, with all its attendant corruption.

Under either monopolistic private direction of production or under the bureaucracy of paternal, and too often tyrannical, government, there is no recognition of the individual and his natural rights of "life, liberty and the pursuit of happiness."

There is a third and entirely different approach to working out the economic needs of all the people. This is the approach that recognizes that power of all kinds corrupts and therefore the society free of corruption and criminality is the society with the widest dispersal of power.

The time has come for the people, all the people, to demand that the nation's entire economy be incorporated---making every citizen a dividend-receiving and voting stockholder. It is long overdue that the people should not only be given a stake *within* the nation but a stake *in* the nation's full capability to produce everything to abundance. Every new-born child has a valid claim against all raw resources and the whole development of technology from the crudest tools to present automated industries.

The heart and substance of a *Corporate Commonwealth* is a complete dispersal of power---creating a society free of crime and corruption---and providing each and every citizen with a valid claim against all goods and services.

People need not endure increasing burdens and mental anguish. They possess the inherent power to liberate themselves from both!

U THANT on EDUCATION IN A CHANGING WORLD

" . . . the search for new, valid and acceptable standards of behavior is the basic problem in international relations, as well as in private life. It is not merely that life without such standards will become increasingly disagreeable and sterile; there is a very real danger that without them we may one day find that human society will cease to be tolerable at all. Of course, education by itself cannot build a new framework of ethics and morals. But it can be of crucial importance in showing the importance of the problem and in providing the atmosphere in which people can work such a framework out for themselves.

"Only an objective, independent and inquiring attitude can hope to succeed in the search for the basic concepts and the underlying principles which can serve the needs of humanity in this century. Such a search, it seems to me, is most likely to end in a sharing and harmonizing of our beliefs.

"It seems to me that education should try to make it possible for people to see beyond the political propaganda and mutual accusations of rival political ideologies to the fundamental values and ideals upon which the conflicting ideologies can be brought together."

The Journal, June 1967 --- The United Church of Christ

~ 38 ~

The Intruder --- Political Zionism

THIS magazine has been asked many times in the past four years to deal editorially with the creation of the state of Israel. In particular, the editors have been requested to express their views on political Zionism. Today, with the entire Middle East in a state of tragic disruption, and the focus of the whole world on this area as a precarious inderbox that could spark World War III, we feel incumbent upon us to deal candidly with the situation.

Certainly, one can now voice observations and draw conclusions without confronting unwarranted charges that one is engaged in some form of "anti-Semitism." In light of the fact that both Arab and Jew are Semitic, any such charge would indeed be ridiculous.

Nevertheless, this writer can attest personally to the fact that cries of "bigotry" and "racial prejudice" inevitably arise when any person is so audacious as to question any abnormal power exercised by elements of Jewry. While no fair-minded person can possibly justify indicting anyone because of his race or religion, at the same time no race can find justification in making false counter-charges of "race discrimination" when substantiated indictment is made against certain elements or individuals of that race.

It is quite proper for Jews to worship at their "wailing wall" to fulfill religious persuasions, but it is quite improper for those same Jews to use it as a sounding board for decrying all those who find Jews not without guilt. Such counter-action is purposely designed to divert public attention from the truth of criminal allegation.

With this preface, let us consider the Middle East.

Applying Same Yardstick

This publication can see no consistency on the part of those who purportedly are for "self-determination," of peoples---devoid of outside interference and exploitation---in Vietnam but at the same time fail to apply this same yardstick to the Israeli-Palestine circumstance.

This publication wants none of such political equivocation. It considers the British, American and political Zionist intrusion in the Arab world just as wrong, just as unjust, just as untenable, as it considers the French and American-Saigon intrusion in the land of the Vietnamese. In both cases the native people are the victims of ruthless and imperialistic intruders!

It indeed seems strange that Senator Morse, et al., have such difficulty in seeing that there exists an almost identical background to the rise of the outside-oriented regime of Saigon and the rise of the outside-oriented state of Israel. The history, the barbarism and the illegality of both are analogous. In neither tragic situation can there be a just and lasting solution until there is accurate and realistic recognition of original and historical causes.

The French for 70 years were the oppressors of the whole area of Indo-China which included both North and South Vietnam. During World War II the Vietnamese fought on the side of the Western Allies but all of the promises to give the Vietnamese their independence were betrayed. In 1954 the Vietminh defeated the French and the resultant Geneva Accords provided for complete withdrawal of the French and the reunification of both North and South Vietnam by elections to be held in 1956.

Unable successfully to sustain the French and prevent their defeat, this nation adopted an approach designed to thwart the victorious Vietnamese from achieving their goal of a colonial-free and independent nation. Our approach was simply to establish and support a pseudo-government, which by the lure of political spoils would serve as an imperialistic beachhead. Thus immediately in 1954 we maneuvered to foist on the South Vietnam people the colonial-oriented regime of Saigon. Since that time to the present, this nation has spent tens of billions of dollars, transported over 500,000 troops and sacrificed over 40,000 lives to perpetuate an artificial created political entity that does not represent the native people of Vietnam.

Uncanny Parallel

This quick recapitulation of the Vietnamese situation should reveal the uncanny parallel with the Middle East Situation. Only identifications are different. Instead of the French, it was the Turks for six centuries and the British for two decades who were the oppressors of the Arab area which included Palestine. Instead of the French, it was the British who promised the Arabs their independence but betrayed the Arabs by bowing to the dictates of the Rothschild's in the Balfour Declaration of 1917.

A more devastating parallel was yet to come. Realizing that the Arabs would relentlessly seek complete independence from foreign domination, and that the Arabs were becoming less tolerant of abusive oil exploitation of their lands, British and American Zionists conceived the approach that was later to be used in Vietnam. This was to set up a pseudo-government in the Arab land that would be an imperialist beachhead in subverting and dominating the Arabs. Such was the genesis of the artificially state of Israel.

In Vietnam, when Saigon was made a puppet of the United States by the setting up of Diem in power, 80% of all the Vietnamese people were in favor of Ho Chi Minh who more truly represented the culture and aspirations of the people. In Palestine, over 90% of the inhabitants were Arabs and the balance were Jews. Yet the preponderant Arabs, like the Vietnamese, had imposed on them a government that likewise did not represent their own culture and aspirations.

"Self-Determination" or Not?

Can anyone be so blind as to not see that neither American-supported Saigon, nor Zionist-supported Israel, represent the native inhabitants over which they rule? Can anyone be so naïve as not to recognize that imperialist domination and economic exploitation underlie the erection of both foreign-dominated governments?

No unprejudiced person can deny the right of every Jew to have political representation in whatever nation he resides. It is also the right of the Jews, as it is with any other people, to make their culture dominant when they as a people are in the preponderance. This is the underlying basis for "self-determination of peoples."

266

However, none of these rights can be exercised so as to preclude the same exercise of these rights by others. The setting up of Israel was in flagrant violation of the rights of "self-determination" belonging to the Arabs. Such violation was perpetuated by the expropriating of the land of the Arabs and the imposing of the Zionist non-indigenous culture on the Arabs. The illegal displacement of over a million Arabs from their homes with attendant suffering compounded the criminal, political aggression of the Zionists against the Arabs of Palestine. Zionism must stand accused as the original perpetrator of aggression in the current Middle East hostilities between Israel and the Arabs.

Political Zionism

Most Americans have innocently and unsuspectingly accepted Zionism as synonymous with Jews and their religion. In particular, Zionism has been accepted as simply an altruistic movement of paternalistic Jews interested in setting up a homeland for the persecuted Jews of the world.

Few Americans recognize that behind this seemingly altruistic goal operated a financial hierarchy of political conspirators representing neither the constructive interests of the preponderant numbers of their own race nor the Arabs nor any non-semitics.

Only students of the history of international banking are aware that long before Zionism emerged with an accepted public identity, there existed a conspiratorial element of Jewry, functioning within the octopus of Rothschild international finance that was carrying on political subversion in every capital of the world. It is imperative in understanding the Middle East situation to realize that it was not the Jews as a race of people but the Zionists who through their entrenchment in the Western Powers set up the state of Israel for ulterior economic and political purposes.

There are many sources revealing the sinister, ruthless record of international Zionism, especially its strangling influence on the governments of the world through its control of international banking. This short article can make no attempt to cover the subject of Zionism. However, we do want to make specific reference to a book entitled *The Rothschild's, A Family Portrait,* which was written by a Jew, Frederic Morton, and published by Atheneum in 1962. Since this book appeared on national best selling lists for months, and since in the preface the author lists the most important Rothschild's in the world as assisting him in corroborating the cited facts, it can hardly be characterized as "anti-Semitic" material.

Rothschild's and Zionism

The story of the Rothschild's starts at the end of the 18th Century with Mayer Amschel Rothschild, a Frankfort money-changer, and covers the intrigue, the manipulations and the ruthlessness of his five sons and their offspring, which not only culminated in the control of the finances of all of Europe but eventually that of the entire world. Perhaps the author best portrays the despotic power the Rothschild's wielded, and continue to wield, when he wrote, in referring to the birthplace of the family, the following amazing paragraph:

"Yet here, in a cramped ghetto dwelling, the great Pauillac wedding had its roots. Here with a yellow star pinned to his caftan, Mayer Amschel Rothschild kept a small store two centuries ago, and married Gutele

Schnapper, and raised with her those five incredible sons who conquered the world more thoroughly, more cunningly and much more lastingly than all the Caesars before or all the Hitlers after them."

However, it is not the incredible story of the Rothschilds and how they toppled governments and pyramided their power over the wealth of the world that concerns us here. Our concern is with the revelation in the book of how the Rothschild's were promoting and financing the Jewish colonization of Palestine even prior to the public identification of Zionism and later were as well the chief collaborators with the Zionists in the setting up the western-oriented state of Israel.

Boastfully and arrogantly, the picture emerges of how it was the ill-gotten Rothschild money, how it was the quiet Rothschild influence behind the governments of the world, and how it was Rothschild plotting that in the accumulate led finally to the setting up of a Zionist political state on the soil of the Arabs.

Aquila strongly recommends the reading of *The Rothschilds* to every one of its readers. In reading the book one is faced with the ironical circumstance that while there has been persecution endured over the centuries by a great number of innocent Jews, at the same time, the most ruthless and callous persecutors the world has ever known is made up of an element in the Jewish people themselves. Neither peace, nor justice, nor constructive social reform can ever be realized for all the races of the world---especially for the common Jews---until the sinister power of financial-political Zionism is broken and eradicated from the earth.

Out of the welter of charges and counter-charges, statements, excuses and evasions that were heard in the tense week of Middle East hostilities, only one American voice faced the issue honestly. A very brief taped interview by Frank McGee with Senator William Fulbright was given on NBC television. The slanted news reports, the attitude of this nation in the UN, and our over-all ambiguous position in the face of Israel's aggression were best explained by Senator Fulbright's unadorned statement that "powerful *Zionist influences* in this nation make it impossible for this nation to be neutral."

Role of the United Nations

Currently, the Middle East situation is before the UN Assembly. World opinion will ultimately force Israel to return the spoils of war. Unfortunately for this nation, we have gained the enmity of the Arab world. If it serves to check our arrogance of power and forces us to look at ourselves introspectively, there could be a by-product of gain. Readjustments must be made by us, as well as by others.

Regrettably, our analysis places us on the side of the Russians, both in regard to Vietnam and the Middle East. No American who loves his country finds it desirable to be so placed. However, proper perspective presents a far different picture. We are not pleading for or holding brief for the Russian system or international policy. Our emphasis is on the wrong courses taken by our own nation which have created vacuums in the world across which Russia and the United States confront each other at the expense of innocent victims abroad and at home.

More and more the United Nations reveals itself as no more constructive and effective than the positions of the Big Powers. It is they who jockey and compromise

270

in their own interests while justice for the small nations, and peace in the world, are only realized as incidental achievements.

However, at the same time, the small nations of the world have their first opportunity to be heard. It is in the context of a platform for the airing of world opinion, where representatives of the smallest and most underdeveloped nations in the world can voice their feelings and aspirations that fully justify the existence of the United Nations.

Voice of Humanity

Excluding the triggering of a nuclear war, Aquila sees some reason to be optimistic in a sadly disrupted and war-torn world. This is not to minimize the devastation in Vietnam with its prolonged agony nor to take only a passing glance at the suffering and heartache in the wake of the Middle East tragedy, nor yet to be blind to the Herculean task yet to be done relating to world disease, hunger and illiteracy. The reason for optimism lies in recognizing that mankind, and here we do not refer to the Big Powers, or the power structures within them, is for the first time exerting itself toward something more constructive and compassionate in human relationships.

Human beings, quite ordinary human beings, are demanding to be considered something other than statistics. Perhaps this drive is best reflected in the emerging nations who for centuries endured oppression and subjugation by those whose only claim to domination lay in their strength of arms and the coercion of their garnered wealth. However, the same drive for emancipation of both body and spirit is exerting itself within the "have" nations. Underlying both is a dynamic de-

271

sire for the right of people as human beings to be the chief arbiters in shaping their own future and that of their children.

It is only when men are free within their own houses that a true Parliament of Man can come into being. The prelude to such achievement has to be complete disarmament by all nations and a subscription to the premise that peace and true profit can only come through mutual cooperation and understanding.

"As a result of the war, corporations have been enthroned and an era of corruption in high places will follow and the MONEY POWER of the country will endeavor to prolong its reign by working on the prejudices of the people until the wealth is aggregated in the hands of a few and the Republic is destroyed. I feel at this moment more anxiety for the safety of my country than ever before, even in the midst of war."

----Abraham Lincoln

~ 39 ~

Humanizing the Artificial Giants! . . .

THIS IS the third article in the series we promised. In dealing with the people's rightful equity in the nation's productive capacity, we are considering the broad outline of an economic framework within which the people's sovereignty could become an actuality and the people could have absolute control of their money supply.

As in the other two articles, much will be left unsaid that in a longer space should be covered. However, our main purpose is served if we succeed in giving new slants, and interjecting new thinking, respecting the three major challenges that confront the nation. We are convinced that there can be no realistic solutions to the serious restraints that burden and strangle the entire nation, until we have the courage and wisdom to free ourselves from unworkable methods.

We at Aquila are not promoting panaceas or "pie in the sky" abstractions. The goals we envision are both workable and attainable. To those to whom our offerings seem radical, we can only emphasize that the problems are radical. To those who are overawed by the magnitude of the problems, or the formidableness of the power structures, we can only stress the need for greater effort by all who seek a better and safer life for all humanity.

Our only regret is the people's slowness in exercising their supreme power. The moment there is a sufficient number of Americans who have an insight as to what changes should be embraced there is no lack of rational leadership to give direction to the enlightened desires of the people.

Economics and Freedom

No one has any difficulty grasping that under European feudalism, when all livelihood came almost exclusively from the land, those who controlled the land were the political masters of the serfs who tilled the soil. The economic well-being and the survival of the people were directly dependent on the whims and concessions of royalty, the landed nobility, and the privileged clergy. For a thousand years the majority of the people slaved and fought for the few who wielded the economic whiplash.

It is this simple relationship of man directly related to his fief, or parcel of land, that it is apparent to all that *political freedom is never any greater than man's economic freedom*. The two are interdependent and directly related. There is no such thing as political freedom when those who control the instruments of production can deny the means of earning a living to those who differ with the views of their economic masters.

The road from the days of European feudalism to modern capitalism is a detailed history of many developments, political, religious and economic. Certainly, there is no room to even highlight such history. However, it is necessary to lay some background in order to

274

broadly grasp how this nation reverted back to another form of feudalism, only it is more intricate and sophisticated. Yet it is as tyrannical politically and as predatory economically.

Founding Fathers

It should not detract from the tremendous stride that our forebears achieved in establishing the first form of popular government to recognize that there were no provisions in the Constitution for the protection of the economic sovereignty of the people. Three circumstances can be cited militating against any real provision for economic justice being incorporated into the Constitution. First, there was unlimited land available for farming, which was the principle means of providing for all economic needs. Secondly, the framers of the Republic were primarily confronted with the task of setting up the first historical experiment in popular government. Thirdly, the nation already harbored powerful landed gentry and was indebted to private financiers, neither of whom would permit restraints to be placed on their abnormal holdings.

Nevertheless, the framers of the Constitution were well aware of the perils that would befall the nation without specific protections against garnered wealth and the control over the means of production by minorities. Many misgivings about the future of the nation were voiced by the most able leaders who brought our nation into being.

James Madison, esteemed as the Father of the Constitution, on August 7, 1987 in the constitutional convention warned as follows: "In future times a great majority of the people will not only be without land, but any other sort of property. These will either combine

275

under the influence of their common situation, in which case the rights of property and the public liberty will not be secure in their hands or, which is more probable, they will become the tools of opulence and ambition, in which case there will be equal danger on another side."

Over thirty years later, Daniel Webster voiced a conclusion for the future that prophetically underscores the predicament of America in the latter part of this twentieth century. He stated as follows: "The freest government, if it could exist, would not long be acceptable, if the tendency of the laws were to create a rapid accumulation of property in a few hands and to render the great mass of the population dependent and penniless. In such a case, the popular power must break in upon the rights of property or else the influence of property must limit and control the exercise of popular power."

Capitalism

Contrary to the belief of many Americans, there was no provision in the Constitution for the economic system we call "capitalism." In fact, it was the absence of any restraints on accumulation of wealth and prohibitions against unearned profits that permitted the vacuum in which the capitalistic system had its beginning. It has been a self-developing and self-perpetuating system that has ultimately led to the tragic circumstance envisioned by Webster almost one hundred and fifty years ago.

While the nation was chiefly agrarian and sprinkled with the self-sustaining small shop, the aspects of "free competition" and "equal opportunity" did maintain to a large degree. However, with the introduction of group endeavor---with the industrial revolution---the built-in

276

flaws of usurious banking and exploitive profit have progressively made a myth of all the idealistic superlatives attributed to capitalism. Right up to the present time it has been a system of economics that has merely given license to the cunning and unscrupulous to exploit the majority.

While most people rightly recognize that communism is the powerful political State controlling the means of production and leaving no room for political sovereignty of the people, few people are willing to face up to the reality that in our own land, capitalism has resulted in a similar subjugation. Under capitalism those who have accumulated the wealth of the nation have made government completely dependent on their wishes and demands. Both systems are predatory and immoral, and have alienated man from his true self.

America today has become a nation whose very lifeblood is vampiristically controlled by a few hundred giant cartels. They are the chief beneficiaries of the nation's resources, its accumulated knowledge, and its technology. The people, the vast majority, have been excluded in both ownership and enjoyment of that which they in the larger measure made possible. Poverty, mass indebtedness and rampant crime are all that they have received not only for their hard work but that of all their forebears.

Scientifically, the nation has made strides but they have been made not because of the system but in spite of it. We have become so overawed by the advancements in communication, transportation and production---with all their attendant gadgetry---that we are unable to encompass the much greater strides that could have been made under an equitable order and a just system of doing the nation's business. We are particularly blind to the inescapable fact that the needs of neither the individual nor the nation are met according to our ability to produce but solely on the basis of how much profit and power will redound to those who own and control the nation's assets and productive potential.

Capitalism is synonymous with the law of the jungle. It is predicated on the erroneous premise that the ability to extract unearned claims against the goods and services of the nation, or to accumulate unearned assets, is sufficient moral justification in itself. If the majority are shortsuited or deprived of that which rightfully belongs to them, neither moral nor ethical responsibility rests with the profiteer, the exploiter or the usurer. It is all condoned and sanctified by camouflaged terms as "free enterprise" and the "free market."

Artificial Entities

Too few people understand that the economic history of this nation has been a continuous, and brutal, struggle between artificial entities, called corporations, and natural entities, which are human beings. The tragedy of that whole history has been that these artificial entities have been created and endowed with powers and privileges far exceeding that of natural persons. As corporations have grown in size, they have ridden roughshod over the rights of natural persons and their constitutional rights to life, liberty and the pursuit of happiness. Thus, the paramount intent of the Constitution to enhance and to protect human rights has been circumvented and destroyed.

The 1965 *Fortune Directory* lists the 500 largest corporations of the 300,000 in the nation. These top 500 manufacturing corporations have assets totaling 224.6 billion dollars. Simple arithmetic reveals that the assets of these 500 *exceed three times* the assets of all the other 299,500 *combined.* And with such concentration of assets goes a parallel concentration of profits and power.

The unmitigated injustice in such concentration lies in the fact that it has been the hard work, the accumulated knowledge, and the resources of the entire nation which have gone into the building of these monopolies, while ownership has been lodged in the hands of major stockholders making up less than five percent of the entire population. It has been the majority of citizens who have paid the "fixed prices" which in turn have furnished the exorbitant profits by which to build bigger and better monopolies. It has been this power *to tax* the consumer to underwrite the expansion of monopoly without giving the consumer any equity in the resultant giant enterprises that underscores the inequity of the capitalistic system.

Into the people's thinking must come the realization that under an equitable and just economic order, no person or group of persons can take from an economy more than they contributed. Conversely, no person or group of persons can be denied their right to enjoy the full fruits of their labor or access to their rightful equity in the nation's whole productive capability. Where then does the answer lie for setting up a framework for preventing the one and realizing the other?

Corporate Commonwealth

Ironical and paradoxical as it may seem to the average person, whereas the corporate structure has been the economic entity by which a minority has been able to usurp ownership and control of the major assets, it at the same time is the most workable pattern by which a whole citizenry could democratically provide for all its material and cultural needs. It is only a question of humanizing the artificial structure by making every citizen a voting stockholder in a national corporation. As stockholders in a *corporate commonwealth,* all profits can accrue to all citizens in the way of dividends.

The quickest way of grasping the practical workings of such incorporation is to take the largest manufacturing corporation in the United States, General Motors, and expand its operations to encompass the entire business of the nation. Bearing in mind that General Motors has an annual business turnover exceeding that of the State of New York, including New York City, and bearing in mind that all giant corporations are in an accelerated process of buying up unrelated industries, it should not be difficult to envision a nationwide incorporation of all production and services. In fact, any projection into the future under present circumstances reveals a trend that can only lead to the ultimate swallowing up of all enterprises by the one most powerful cartel, anyway.

The question to be confronted is simply this: At what point do the entire citizenry become the rightful owners and beneficiaries of the national productive plant which all the people made possible? How long can the people as consumers be made to pay the administered prices in a noncompetitive economy that underwrite the expanding and merging of monopolies without themselves having any ownership? How long can the people as taxpayers be made to pay for multi-billion dollar contracts and research programs which only increase the dominance of the select monopolies without themselves receiving any equity?

As monopolies become bigger, with constant employment of more automated machines to do the work, the American people as workers, consumers and taxpayers are actually in the idiotic business of paying for their exclusion from the entire economy. The only avenue given them has been to go into astronomical, hopeless debt. Current figures show that right now the increasing rate of indebtedness exceeds that of the increasing rate of productivity!

Any child knows that one cannot take out of the barrel more than he puts in. Yet, just the opposite concept underlies our present indebtedness-productivity ratio.

The crux of the nation's whole economic problem has nothing to do with the bigness of coordinated industries. It has nothing too do with automation and cybernation as application of our best technology to do work. It has everything to do with employing and directing that bigness and technology for the full benefit of a nation of 190,000,000 citizens. This can only be achieved by making every citizen a dividend-receiving stockholder based on an equity that he has already earned, directly or indirectly. Only then can there be a total purchasing power which to buy all that is produced in both goods and services.

If capitalism is to work, then every solitary citizen must be a voting participant in the employment of the nation's assets. Anything less is but a perpetuation of the master-slave arrangement.

Power of the People

It would be the hope of Aquila that sufficient people could be immediately enlightened so that major economic adjustments could be made in a fortnight. However, we entertain no such optimism. There is every probability that the injustice and unworkability of the system must become more apparent before the people demand an accounting. Our concern is in persuading people that the power, legally and within the framework of the Constitution, is in their hands to do it tomorrow if they so desire.

"Life, liberty and property" have been taken from the people without due process of law. In major cases, involving the biggest steel and electrical companies in the nation, the courts have found them, as defendants, guilty of defrauding the public. It is within the realm of court procedure to make all major monopolies disgorge their holdings because they belong to the people.

The taxing power of the government could be constitutionaly used to reduce the "illegal" earnings of the giant cartels. A corporate commonwealth would recognize the sound economic premise that no person should have a claim against goods and services beyond his ability to use or enjoy them personally. At the same time, every person should be constitutionally guaranteed a basic minimum by which to maintain a decent standard of living.

In the broader scope, the nation's whole economy could be incorporated and the people's equity restored in the nation's productive potential by the constitutional provision of Public Domain. If a soldier can be conscripted to give his life because it is interpreted that the nation's *outer* security is at stake, certainly, then,

282

the property of a nation can be "conscripted" to establish the *inner* security of the 190,000,000 citizens within its boundaries.

Right now we are a nation that struggles under a system that is not only bankrupting itself materially but more seriously is bankrupting itself morally and ethically. No system is worth defending or preserving that prevents its citizens from expressing or enlarging their own potentials, whether physical, mental or spiritual.

That is the real indictment of debt-burdening and crime-encouraging capitalism!

"A popular Government, without popular information, or the means of acquiring it, is but a Prologue to a Farce or a Tragedy; or, perhaps both. Knowledge will forever govern ignorance. And a people who mean to be their own Government, must arm themselves with the power which knowledge gives."

---James Madison

~ 40 ~

What's Wrong with Economic Planning?

F EW DISCUSSIONS are held which don't sooner or later run into communication barriers because of the different meanings given to certain words. Somewhere during the dialog between participants there invariably arises the need to clarify the meaning of a special word. If the effort is made to clarify it, it is frequently found that the speakers were interpreting the same word or phrase in entirely different ways.

All too often, the effort to clarify definitions is not made, and the discussion deteriorates into empty wrangling, only to break up in hard feelings and total lack of communication. A pre-defining of terms should be a prerequisite to any meaningful exchange or expression of opinion.

Often we hear someone interject, "I think it is possible we agree on this point; it is only the matter of 'semantics' that is involved." In other words, each person has been using the same word but attributing to it a different meaning. What many persons do not yet realize is that there is a growing branch of knowledge called *General Semantics* in which it has been discovered that certain words or phrases, of and by themselves, evoke strong emotional responses. Often the individual is unable to account for his emotional reaction which has no direct association with the word in question. More often, however, it can be accounted for by lack of information or by prejudicial resentments.

It is in light of the foregoing that we want to deal in this article with the phrase "planned economy." Not only are there diametrically opposed meanings associated with the phrase, but its mere usage emotionally upsets many people. This writer has found persons who either mentally freeze or else explode whenever the words are uttered. They react as if they had suddenly been asked to join the Communist party or brand each newborn child with a serial number of identification. If they learn that the Corporate Commonwealth idea falls in the scope of "planned economy," they forthwith refuse to listen to one more word on the subject.

First, let us consider the word *planning* or *planned* strictly as to meaning. Consulting a Webster Collegiate Dictionary, we come up with this definition: "To devise or project a method or course of action." No one has any difficulty in applying this definition. Nor does anyone have any difficulty in applying this definition to nearly every aspect of one's personal day-to-day living. It involves every member of the family. The child is taught to plan his schoolwork, his recreation, and his 7:00 p. m. rendezvous with the Beatles at the local theatre.

The mother projects a full course of action involving meals, the washing, attending PTA meetings as well as the other thousand and one chores connected with keeping a family contented and organized. Father has his planned work and is the chief arbiter in spending his weekly paycheck so that the prorated needs of the family can best be fulfilled. Together they lay plans for trips, buying the new home and the college education of the children.

NO ONE questions the need, or the wisdom, of a well-regulated family's engaging in the aforementioned planning. In fact, not only is it accepted as a matter of course, but lack of it is inveighed against as pure shiftlessness. In the final analysis, it is nothing but an attempt to apply intelligence in order to achieve the best result. It is nothing more, nor anything less.

Behold, however, what a different reaction is evoked whenever the question of planning comes up in respect to the running of the national household! By some twisted and inconsistent reasoning any application of planning now becomes inherently wrong, and there is strong emotional rejection, often even precluding discussion.

Our first consideration then is to identify if we can the cause of this initial reaction. In so doing, we discover two propositions or states of mind underlying the surface response to planning in government or in the economic life of the nation. They can be stated as follows:

1. Anything that is "planned" is synonymous with governmental bureaucracy and smacks of foreign "isms."

2. A "free market economy" is what this nation enjoys and any form of economic planning would be detrimental to the well being of the people.

The tragic circumstance is that both of the stated reactions fall largely in the area of "general semantics" and have very little to do with any factual understanding of how our economy functions. If the individual had an analytical grasp of the ownership and control of the nation's productive machinery, he would know that we already live under an absolute *planned* economy. He would realize that it has not been planning of and by itself, but the *absence of intelligent planning,* that has opened the door to all forms of expanding bureaucracy.

Every American should be rightfully indignant over the multitudes of forms and questionnaires coming out of Washington which he is required to fill out. He should rightly object to the constant flow of decrees and fiats that regulate a citizen's every movement. He should be opposed to subsidies, unemployment payments, welfare programs, and the whole gamut of wastrel bureaus supported by tax dollars as any constructive solution to our economic problems.

All of these are but palliatives and regimentation and should be recognized as such. But this is only half of the picture. We are viewing the effects and not the causes compelling government intervention.

THE first thing that must be clear in our minds is that we live under an economy that is planned to the *nth* degree not only in its administration but in achieving its end result. Only the extreme naïve believe that somehow America is still an agrarian nation interspersed with small independent businesses. They are pathetically unaware that only a few hundred corporations despotically determine not only the amount of production, the fixed price of every consumer item, and the number of workers that shall have employment, but that their interest is only in increased profits and power.

Most seriously, these monopolies assume no obligation either to respect the economic rights of the individual, or the well-being and solvency of the nation.

It is because our whole economy is arbitrarily planned for the few that we have millions unemployed, tens of millions living in poverty, a nation spiraling further into hopeless debt, crime alarmingly on the increase, and two million boys and girls entering the labor force each year with no meaningful roles available. It is ridiculous to contend that government bureaucracy is responsible for the economic inequities, and economic breakdown, so overwhelmingly evident.

The reverse is the truth of the circumstance. It is the malfunctioning of our debt-money, predatory economy that has created huge vacuums into which overlording government steps.

The big lesson to be derived from an accurate analysis of the economic problems in the nation and the role of government is that when a nation's economy is *planned badly* such planning is synonymous with bureaucracy. Conversely, when a nation's economy would be *planned soundly* individual liberty would be the least circumscribed by dependence on "handouts" and dictates of government.

THE second lesson to be derived from an honest appraisal of our whole economic structure and how it functions is that we as a nation do not enjoy a "free-market" economy. This is an ideological illusion that has been deliberately promoted as a camouflage behind which the despotic manipulators of our productive machinery rule with absolute power. Less than 300 corporations, owning over two-thirds of all productive assets, control and direct the production of over three-quarters of all goods in the entire nation. Less than ten percent in the nation now fall in the category of the so-called self-employment.

Or another statistical observation is that less than one percent on the top own over 28 percent of all wealth, while the ten percent on the bottom own less than one percent of the wealth. Or, considering all stock ownership, over 95 percent of all stock is in the hands of less than five percent of American families.

However, it is not the concentration of wealth, achieved by denying the people their rightful equity, or the bigness of operation, that most seriously concern us. It is the concentration of financial and industrial power in the hands of the few who deliberately plan built-in obsolescence and scarcity that they might realize the maximum profits. This leads to further expansion of holdings and increased concentration of power.

Translated into human considerations we observe a nation with the technology and resources to provide more in the way of all goods and services than could be humanly used condemning tens of millions to poverty and lack of medical needs, and driving the young into crime. Out of such irreconcilable conditions are bred anarchy and the collapse of society.

A TECHNOLOGICAL society such as we have today cannot be premised on a "dog-eat-dog" approach with unlimited spoils going to the strong. Survival of the fittest worked in this nation when the weak had the opportunity to move westward to open new territory. No longer is this possible. Within the confines of the nation's borders the people must find solutions that deal directly with all the nation's tools, natural resources, technology and manpower. There is no escape.

Up to this point in our history, all progress has been primarily geared to a science of material things. The new order to be introduced must be the science of human beings. Belatedly, it must be recognized that man was not meant to serve technology, but that our best science and institutions should serve man. Man was not intended to be the slave of the things he perfects. This has come about only because it has been to the profit of a minority to so subordinate the inherent rights of human beings.

We at Aquila do not object to an economy that is planned. What we are advocating is an economy that is planned for the majority of the people. To those who are emotionally upset by the use of the word "planned," we would gladly substitute the phrase "coordinated economy." In fact, it more accurately identifies the social reform we propose. We simply advocate the intelligent *coordination* of all phases of our economy so that there can be maximum utilization of our productive potential in providing the maximum good life for all of the people.

When you fully understand the central goal of the Corporate Commonwealth Idea, you will grasp that it simply plans the economic framework within which every individual can live life completely unplanned by bureaucrats and power-blocs!

That is its one and only goal!

~ 41 ~

The Rights With Which You Are Born

At THIS TIME we come to consider the most important premises, or fundamentals, that underlie all human relationships and social structure. We come to consider the rights every human being is born with, irrespective of location, parental means, or the color of his skin. To understand these inherent rights is to possess the bedrock yardsticks with which not only to evaluate inequities existing in prevailing laws, economic and political arrangements, and institutions, but to shape such social reform as will be just to every member in organized society.

Every student of history is familiar with scholars of government and economic reform who championed the "rights of man" from the time of Plato to the present time. Unfortunately, few are such students who fully grasp what the Platos, the John Lockes, the Rousseaus, the Tom Paines, the Bellamys and the William Dudley Pelleys were basically endeavoring to convey. The problem lies in the failure to read what these champions of human rights offered in the context of the times in which they wrote. These reformers, from a strictly practical standpoint, were compelled to advocate the rights of the individual in light of the productive techniques, the communication facilities,

291

the political systems then existing. The exercise of inherent rights were not only limited by actual physical circumscriptions but then, as now, political and economic power-blocks held the majority in a state of servitude.

The uncanny thing is the consistency with which the rights of man have been pleaded up the centuries. It is also noteworthy to appreciate that all these advocates of social change, seeking the more wholesome and equitable life have had to endure persecution at the hands of the despotic forces whose abnormal influence was in direct ratio to the injustice meted out to the struggling majority. So it is today. Yet, there can be no meaningful roles in society until there is full recognition of the inalienable rights of every human being who enters life.

The first important thing to grasp is that human rights don't change from age to age, or from generation to generation. Only the scope of their exercise increases along with man's improvement of the tools with which to meet his needs and fulfill his urges. His rights to live, to act, to perform, to learn, and to enjoy life are constant and remain the same. They are irrevocable laws of Nature that are inviolate to every person.

The second important inescapable fact that must be accepted is that every human being enters life with exactly the same rights as any other human being. No person enters life with more rights. No person enters life with fewer rights. There are no designated favorites. The Creator of the Universe is impartial in his endowments of basic human rights to each and every individual. It has been the greed, and lust for power, of man against man that has fashioned rules and institutions which have destroyed the inherent rights of so many countless millions.

In THE LAST ISSUE of *The Eagle's Eye* we endeavored to present broadly the premise that we live in a good and rational Universe. Chiefly we wanted every person to get the full impact of the fact that no person comes into life with tools or raw stock but that he has a rightful claim against both upon his arrival. We emphasized the fact that all raw ingredients, from the trees that make up the forests, the minerals found beneath the ground, the oceans as unlimited reservoirs of wealth, and every cubic inch of atoms fraught with nuclear energy awaiting release, are the building-blocks of Nature belonging to all the people. Simultaneously, we emphasized that no individual, or group of individuals, has any priority on the accumulated knowledge to which so many billions of people have directly, and indirectly, contributed since the caveman discovered the first machine principles to do work. This, too, is a legacy of all the people.

It is with this background firmly in mind that we commenced to give serious thought to the specific rights of every individual. And what is the most basic right of every new-born baby? It is the right to life itself! To this every sentimentalist will give three lusty cheers! After offering some pious platitudes about unswerving allegiance to protecting babyhood, he will feel that all has been said that is necessary on the subject. The more cynical will make asinine remarks about the irresponsibility of parents who bring young ones into the world but who can't provide for their needs. Neither viewpoint meets the challenge foursquare. Meanwhile, the millions of children living in squalor, crying for food, and in need of medical care in the nation's slum areas and Appalachia's have few rights that find meaningful expression.

A society that was predicated on inherent rights of every individual would recognize that while the infant born has no ability to fend for itself, it has an automatic claim, or credit, against the natural resources and accumulated knowledge. Such inherited credit exceeds what is required to meet all the needs of the child until he assumes his adult role in society. No child could thus be denied adequate nourishing food, all needed medical attention, or the full underwriting of his education. What valid argument can be given that one child is not as important as another? Or the one child's claim is not as great to life as another?

Of course adults have the same claim, or credit, against which to demand their rightful share in all natural resources and contributions of past science to current knowledge. However, in the case of grown people, we can spell out the nature of such stake in more specific terms relating to inherent rights. In contrast to helpless children, adults can play literal roles in working out of all material needs, and the functioning of government.

It IS DIFFICULT to present in limited space all the ramifications of the inherent rights of every person. As stated earlier these rights do not take on meaning unless one translates them into definitive areas of expression. Broadly, all inherent rights fall into two major categories:

1. The constant right to expend maximum effort for the well-being of oneself and one's family.

2. The constant right to participate in all aspects and decisions affecting one's role in society.

The first determines man's economic security, and the second determines man's political security. In the first instance we are concerned simply with how well man survives in direct ratio to his nation's ability to produce all material things. In the second instance, we are concerned simply with the sovereignty of the people and the right of every solitary individual to be a participant in society in direct ratio to his innate talents. Let us consider them independently for a few paragraphs.

When the nation was first founded, there were few restrictions on the new citizen's right to expend maximum effort to obtain a livelihood for himself and his family. There was unlimited virgin territory and man's productive capacity was primarily his own hands and a strong back. He cleared the land, planted his seeds, and harvested his crops as a self-sustaining enterprise. That which he produced beyond his needs, he exchanged with neighbors for goods of which they had excess. This was an exchange of value for value, through simple barter, and to all intents and purposes the nation's first citizens did have equal access to natural resources, and they could exercise the right to expend maximum effort for the well being of their families.

"Private enterprise" at this point of the nation's history had real meaning and did enhance the inherent rights of the individual. It was an entirely new concept in economic arrangement, the right of every individual to his personal piece of property, or small shop, and it was meaningful liberation from the feudalistic landlord-tenant system of Europe. What the founding fore-fathers were unable to foresee was that the unre-stricted "right to private property" would revert back to a similar form of industrial capitalistic feudalism more unjust than that from which they had escaped.

In Europe the majority worked for those who had cor-ralled and owned the land. Since the human element was indispensable, it was necessary that the workers be fed and given at least a pittance for their labor. Ultimately, the time would arrive in America, as it exists today, when the majority would be working for those who would corral and own all the nation's pro-ductive assets and machinery. However, in contrast to the feudalism of Europe where the tenant was needed, the current industrial, or capitalistic feudalism, does not need the worker. Machines can perform increas-ingly all operations.

IN PAST ARTICLES, we have endeavored to present to you the built-in evils of private issuance and manip-ulation of the nation's money, or credit, and the un-bridles aggregating of the nation's productive capacity into the hands of fewer and fewer owners. Our chief concern in this article is to emphasize the inherent right of every person, irrespective of his birth or mater-ial means, to enjoy his rightful share of all resources, technology and productive capability. It is the right to material security that is important and not the methods that have become outmoded along with in-creased knowledge and the perfecting of tools.

No longer is it the piece of private property that is im-portant but a positive claim against the entire national productive machinery which can make maximum use of our most advanced technology to produce everything to abundance. Each person must now have, not a stake *within* the nation, but a stake *in* the nation. Understand this basic difference, and you will grasp that private ownership has simply been translated into a realistic, meaningful, part-ownership of the whole. Thus your right to expend maximum effort in refining raw stock into useable goods makes you a direct beneficiary of the maximum utilization of machines to do work.

You are a perpetual, cooperative shareholder in the whole nation!

WE NOW COME to consider man's inherent right *to participate* in all aspects of society. Whereas this right embodies the right to expend effort for material well being, it encompasses the whole spectrum of the individual's role in organized human relationships. Not only does every human being have a God-given right to develop his own particular talents to the utmost, but he has a sovereign right, along with all other individuals, to participate directly in the functioning of all social structures, economic and political, which affect his well being and promote his betterment.

Again we must consider the right to participate in the same vein as we did man's right to work. Circumstances of the past were not what they are today. The Founding Fathers escaped from the political concept of "the Divine Right of Kings" and set up a constitutional Republic wherein the people directed government by representatives. Because of both transportation and communication barriers this was the only feasible exercise of the people's sovereignty. As with unlimited "right to private property," so has "delegation of power" become outmoded with the advances in communication that place all people in instant contact with each other.

Along with strides in education, more especially the potential of education, coupled with the leisure time that will be at everyone's disposal, there can be no further toleration of turning over to professional politicians the basic role of governing. When economically liberated, the most important business at hand will be the direct running of government by the people themselves. There will be no need for machine-controlled political parties. All candidates will be candidates of the people, elected to fill offices for recommending laws or policies upon which a supreme people make the final decision. This is not only the safest exercise of power but affords participation that develops the character and self-reliance of every citizen.

At this point it should be apparent that freedom to express, to publish, to follow one's own religious persuasion, to petition government, and the other provisions contained in the Bill of Rights are all supplementary to the categories covered. As such they should not be minimized. They are automatically included in the role of every citizen when he enjoys full benefit from the nation's material potential, and the people enact their own laws and administer their equitable execution.

The same goes for the *right to peace*. When the peoples of all nations play their parts as dynamic and meaningful participants in their respective societies, there will be no more wars. Good will and peace will have become a natural reality.

Every human being is a product of a Creator who has endowed him with the same inherent rights as any other human being. The exercise of such inherent rights must be in direct ratio to the maximum tools, knowledge and wisdom possessed by all the people at any given time in history.

Apply the foregoing to evaluating the current prohibitive restraining and dangerous environment in which mankind now struggles and the need to free man becomes a compelling challenge.

How quickly, and how effectively, we meet that challenge will denote recognition of our own birthright!

A people who exercise their inherent rights are indomitable!

~ 42 ~

The Seven Deadly P's

By *Adelaide Pelley Pearson*

On BEING asked the other day what we considered to be the greatest menaces of happiness on the current scene, we discovered that our answers came like corn popping---it seems that most of the words describing the problems begin with the letter "P".

Population explosion, poverty, pollution, police state, polarization. Even the results of monopoly in the tired, old "military-industrial complex" exploded into the ancient but fitting word, "plutocracy."

Having accepted this odd and irrelevant phonetic fact as a challenge, we were momentarily stumped by one of the worst menaces of all---war and all its ghastly train of destruction, real and threatened, conflict itself, hot or cold, preparedness for a nuclear war which is un-thinkable, and the possible accidents resulting from such horrendous activity in the way of mislaid H-bombs, improperly controlled nerve gases and the possible escape of germs so lethal that there is no known cure. But we weren't stopped for long. We coined a word that covers the problem to our satis-faction: *"Pentagony"* with accent on the second syllable.

Out of the plethora of problems that imperil us, we chose the seven worst (in our opinion) to keep per-nicious company with the Seven Deadly Sins. There is no point in trying to set them down in the order of their importance. Each has its own application to individual circumstance and to the whole scene as well. We'll just take 'em as they come.

Plutocracy: Government by the wealthy says the dictionary. So obviously is this a fact of modern life that it hardly needs mentioning. Two comments must be made, however. First, so thoroughly has the American public been propagandized into measuring success in terms of money that a plutocracy seems to most Americans not only natural but eminently respectable and desirable. Second, most Americans accept this propaganda because they are not yet aware that the good old American traditions of "equal opportunity" and "free enterprise" have long since become myths, with no application to today's harsh reality.

With a handful of Horatio-Alger exceptions (widely publicized by those who benefit from the perpetuation of the myth) the rule of "them that has, gits!" has never worked so well. Never has old Amschel Meyer Rothschild's dictum, "I care not who makes the laws; let me control the purse strings," been so gloriously illuminated. A day of accounting is coming for which we must be prepared.

Poverty: This the other end of the same stick. As a system which glorifies property at the expense of human beings continue on its unthinking and self-aggrandizing way, in this most affluent of nations, some people starve while others are paid fabulous sums not to produce food, the prices of all things rise, pinching the consumer painfully, or forcing him to go without altogether, while "administered prices" far exceeding all costs so that "profit is maximized" and their principle stockholders continue to get their lucrative

301

dividends; and the only way offered to stem the constant devaluation of our money is to "slow business down" by raising interest rates to unheard of heights, with the result that homes desperately needed are not built, the ordinary citizen cannot get what he needs without going ever further into debt, and a rise in unemployment is regarded as a healthy indication that "inflation is being curbed."

In short, while the rich are getting richer, the poor are getting desperate. When middle-class Americans, who pay the freight for both, finally get the message, belatedly they will evince more disposition toward major social reform. They now smugly judge their security by the number of people of much lesser income below them.

Police State: Already the wrath of the most disadvantage of our citizens, the blacks, is being felt. Already the brightest of our young people who have the imagination and the brains to see and understand the handwriting on the wall are making their scorn and disgust felt. Already taxpayers are beginning to discuss organization against such wholesale exploitation and their protests will soon be felt. Sadly, all this justified indignation against back-breaking taxes is as yet fragmented: against taxes for war and destruction; against taxes for foreign aid that does not aid; against taxes covering a pure nightmare of "welfarism"; against the arbitrary dictates of the Federal Reserve and its allied private banks. Taxpayers do not yet understand that all of these very real irritations are rooted in a "system" that takes the " maximization of profit" as its No. 1 responsibility and looks on human beings only as statistics or numbers in a computer. Sooner or later, they will become aware.

But those who control the computers and deal with the statistics are worried, too. The atmosphere of dissatisfaction, protest, dissent, and revolt brought on by the inequities of the system bids fair to burst into open flame---even worse than has already occurred. Those who run the system, who are profiting by it, who want it to continue without change, see in these smoldering areas of discontent a threat to the way they want things to be. Their only recourse (or they think so) is to put down these dissenters, prosecute them, fine them, jail them, discredit them, and silence them somehow, anyhow. "Law and Order" becomes the topic of the day. Its rightful concomitant, Justice, is forgotten, overlooked, ignored. So the power of the police, of the judiciary or the military is invoked to serve a tottering status quo.

How tragic it is that these would-be preservers of an old order (many of them of excellent intent) cannot recognize the changes that technological ingenuity has created; that they cannot see how the world has grown smaller while humans needs increase; that the safety valves on the old system have all been blown and a new era in human relationships and human activity is bearing down on us all. A police state is a menace at this moment---but it can be only a temporary, although painful and quite possibly bloody, obstacle in the path to a new and freer age.

Pentagony: The warfare state is akin to the police state but more perilous to mankind generally because of the horrifying nature of the gadgets it is playing with. War is still acceptable to older hands, out of habit. War has always been the ultimate way to settle all international disagreements. There are many older mentalities that have not yet grasped that nuclear war

303

means total and complete annihilation of the human race and very likely the planet itself. Inhibited and crystallized minds are capable of saying if only two people are left on earth to start civilization anew, "I want them to be Americans!" Unfortunately, such minds are to be found in high seats of government where their brainstrapped decisions seriously affect your survival and mine.

There are other minds, not just in the Pentagon but on Capitol Hill and in the boardrooms of great corporations across the land that are blinded by the golden flow of money to the red flow of American blood into rice paddies and onto jungle floors.

"War will exist until that distant day when the conscientious objector enjoys the same reputation and prestige that the warrior does today," said John F. Kennedy. When the American people begin to be ashamed of what the Pentagon represents instead of glorying in it, we shall begin to make progress toward a safer world.

Pollution: We chose this word to cover a multitude of abuses that are threatening our survival far more seriously than we are conscious of. More and more people are becoming aware that Lake Erie has been ruined, perhaps past praying for. More and more people are becoming aware that the indiscriminate use of DDT and other chemicals are beginning to constitute a real peril to human life instead of just to the insects they were meant to control. But all too few people are aware of the subtler dangers about which the ecologists are trying to warn us. The loss of vital "wilderness" areas which we must have if we are to learn how to survive in the future; the indiscriminate building of dams, bridges, roads, power stations, jetports, reservoirs, all designed to "further progress" but which, because of pure ignorance or a "public-be-damned" attitude, are in reality endangering human survival; the unplanned, unthinking sprawl of cities, the befouling of streams, lakes, air and ground with the waste products of our highly touted technological society; the noise, the dirt, the crowding and the ugliness that is warping us all; the callous indifference or the incredible shortsightedness of the profit-makers who cause these problems, yet refuse to pay the price to have them corrected or avoided---these area problems that all of us can look into, be concerned with and take action on. And we had better do so quickly, since our lives depend upon it. We shall, of course, have to keep foremost in our minds that what is good for business is not always good for the human race.

There is another area of pollution not usually categorized as such. This is the pollution of the human body by stimulants, tranquilizers, supposedly therapeutic but unproven drugs, in addition to the increasing use of psychedelic or additive drugs and the misuse of alcohol. Most of these pollutants of the human body are used simply as desperate and dangerous escape mechanisms from the pressures of a society that are too much for frail spirits to cope with.

A society that encouraged the individual instead of disadvantaging him, that enhanced his best characteristics instead of exciting or appealing to his worst, that respected his efforts at self-improvement instead of ridiculing or ignoring them, would find the escape mechanisms of drugs and alcohol losing their appeal and becoming eventually of minimal consequence.

Population Explosion: Our problem in the United States today is not too many people over all, as yet, but too many people crowded into too few living areas. This is a problem that is yet solvable by the use of considerable native ingenuity *plus* the release of purchasing power from destructive to constructive ends. But for future generations, demographers (those who study population as a science) are generally agreed on one of two essentialities. Either the population will be decimated by the disaster of nuclear war or worldwide plague or famine, or there will come a time all too soon when there will literally be nowhere to go. *Unless* we put our minds to it and begin to make headway in the education necessary. It will be only a matter of time before the Catholic Church begins to take a realistic view, but it is an ironic fact that sensible birth control is practiced now largely among the intelligent and the affluent, those who are able to produce, and provide best for, healthy babies. The illiterate and the ignorant breed rapidly, and since medical science continues to save and prolong life, the problem mounts. The only answer is education, education and more education if disaster is to be avoided in this area.

Polarization: This is the Personal Peril. This is the one menace that is an individual responsibility, the one problem that a human being may battle single handed, after he has fought it out in his own heart.

The great exhortation of the day is to become "committed." Being committed beats apathy every time. At worst, it keeps you from being bored and gives you a comfortable sense of righteousness. At best, you join the ranks of saints and martyrs.

306

But commitment to any cause has its negative dangers. All too often those committed consider themselves to have a corner on the Truth, the only true pipeline to God. All too often the extent of their commitment is to the eradication (not only figuratively but literally) of whomsoever they don't like.

It is sometimes hard to keep in mind that we're all in this thing together.

Frustration contending against apathy breeds excess. Excess on one side breeds excess on the other. Confrontation on any level, white against black, antiwarriors against "patriots," left against right, whatever the cause, makes a few martyrs and stirs vicious backlash. Everybody shouts and nobody listens.

This is polarization: the inability or the willingness to hear the other side, to recognize the basic needs of any portion of humanity, to realize the overwhelming and primary demand to work out relationships that will benefit *all* citizens, not just one aggrieved portion, no matter how justified the grievance.

Now, if ever, as man prepares for the first time to set foot on another planet in space, should we realize how small our earth is, how like to a spaceship it is, floating through the limitless ocean of the universe, and how incumbent it is upon us to recognize our common humanity to "get along," our common need to stop destroying each other and thereby ourselves, and by taking a little thought, find out if it is not possible to create a life and a society on this small planet that we can enjoy. In the face of our marvelous potentials, what tempest in teapots we create for ourselves!

307

So we have played our grim little game with the letter "P". It must be noted that the letter "P" has its positive aspects as well: Peace instead of Pentagony, Plenty instead of Poverty, People's power instead of Plutocracy. You can play your own game, but be sure you take it seriously.

Survival depends on it!

~ 43 ~

Man Could Say "It Is Good" Once Too Often

From **Farmland,** October 15, 1968

IN THE END, there was Earth, and it was with form and beauty.

And man dwelt upon the lands of the Earth, the meadows and trees, and he said,

"Let us build our dwellings in this place of beauty with concrete and steel.

And the meadows were gone.

And man said, "It is good."

On the second day, man looked upon the waters of the Earth,

And man said, "Let us put our waste in the waters that the dirt can be washed away."

And man did.

And the waters became polluted and foul in their smell.

And man said, "It is good."

On the third day, man looked upon the forests of the Earth and saw they were beautiful.

And man said, "Let us cut the timber for our homes and grind the wood for our use.

And man did. And the lands became barren and the trees were gone.

And man said, "It is good."

On the fourth day, man saw that animals were in abundance and ran in the fields and played in the sun.

And man said, "Let us rage these animals for our own amusement and kill them for our sport."

And man did. And there were no more animals on the face of the earth.

On the fifth day, man breathed the air of the Earth.

And man said, "Let us dispose of our wastes into the air for the winds shall blow them away."

And man did. And the air became filled with the smoke and the fumes could not be blown away.

And the air became heavy with dust and choked and burned.

And man said, "It is good."

On the sixth day, man saw himself, and seeing many languages and tongues, he feared and hated.

And man said, "Let us build great machines and destroy these, lest they destroy us."

And man built great machines, and the Earth was fired with the rage of great wars.

And man said, "It is good."

On the seventh day, man rested from his labors and the Earth was still for . . .

Man no longer dwelt upon the Earth.

And it was good.

~ 44 ~

In the Throes of Revolution

THE NATION is in the throes of revolution. It has come full cycle since it's founding. Once again, human beings as human beings are sounding the tocsin that they cannot be subordinated to property or institutions.

The revolution setting up this nation was the action of a people freeing themselves economically from feudal-istic ownership of the means of livelihood and politi-cally from the "divine right of kings." The dynamics of that revolution were clearly enunciated in the Declara-tion of Independence. It was to be the bedrock premise upon which a new social order would be erected insur-ing the sovereign people, every solitary individual, of being the chief beneficiaries of the nation's efforts.

Unfortunately, the paramount importance of human beings and the absolute sovereignty of the people were not sufficiently spelled out in the Constitution, nor were sufficient safeguards included, to make possible the people being the arbiters of their lives and their destinies. Yet the principle of popular government had been introduced and a major stride away from feudal-ism and self-perpetuated royalties had been achieved. However, before two centuries would pass the nation would revert back to a new form of feudalism and po-litical subservience, equally tyrannical, only more sophisticated and subtle.

311

The current revolution is a revolution of human beings against the artificial entities of a military-industrial-financial-political complex that have made greed and the power of the Almighty Dollar more important than the love and survival of man. Thus, the underlying drive of the current revolution must be the re-shaping of our institutions and government so that the corrupting influence of power can be removed from all aspects of the society. But the revolution must go further.

It must be a revolution of giving each individual, of whatever skin-color or nationality, his rightful stake in the full productive capacity of the nation. The American Revolution made man part of Nature by the availability of ample land. The New Revolution must renew man's partnership with Nature by giving him equal equity in the potential of energy and accumulated technology.

With economic sovereignty must come political sovereignty. Economic injustice and perpetual involvement in needless and brutal wars have taken too harsh a toll for the sovereign people to allow the decision-making power to be delegated. Henceforth, every individual must have a positive and final voice on all decisions that affect his well-being and future.

What is unique about the current revolution in America is that it is the first revolution of the people within an industrial society. All revolutions to date, including and following the American Revolution, have taken place in agrarian societies. The French Revolution, shortly after our own, and the revolutions of this century in Russia, China and Cuba have all been people's revolutions against landed aristocracies within predominantly agricultural nations.

These countries have yet to become as highly industrialized as America. Only time will reveal whether they will go the route of this nation with the progressive emergence of power structures as they transform from agrarian societies to technological ones. This seems to be the case in Russia where there is such similarity between its State Capitalism of political dominance and our Private Capitalism of economic dominance.

The dynamics of the current revolution must come from an understanding of the restraints on society and more importantly a vision of the goals that would mean liberation, justice and a safe society. The true leadership of the revolution will recognize that while it is easier to arouse the hate emotion against tangible government, institutions, and conditions of injustice, the more powerful love emotion can be brought into play by dynamically giving the people constructive goals that are attainable. The only hate should be for the "system" which has no potential to change itself. Only compassion should be felt for those whom the system has corrupted and who possess the capacity to change and perform altruistically.

The dynamics of the present revolution must, through understanding, rest on the irrepressible desire of people to be free. Such desire, however dormant, resides in the breast of every human.

Awaken it and it will engender its own momentum toward final achievement of all goals that *unshackle the body, the mind and the spirit of all human beings.*

The Limits of Tyranny

Frederick Douglass
(West India Emancipation Speech, August 1857

"Power concedes nothing without demand. Find out just what any people will quietly submit to and you have found out the exact measure of injustice and wrong which will be imposed upon them, and these will continue till they are resisted with either words or blow, or with both.

"The limits of tyrants are prescribed by the endurance of those whom they oppress."

* * * * *

"Those who make peaceful revolution impossible, will make violent revolution inevitable."

---John F. Kennedy

Walter Pearson

May 9, 1912 – November 1, 1995

He was a social activist all his life. His main focus was on the supreme power of the sovereign people. His efforts were on all levels of government---Local, State and Federal---where he relentlessly and uncompromisingly challenged the usurped power of the nation's most abusive giant economic and financial corporations.

He offered proposals that would unleash our full work capability and would achieve an equitable and prosperous society with full implementation of the constitutional and inherent rights of every solitary person.